ORIENTAL THOUGHT

An Introduction to the Philosophical and Religious Thought of Asia

ORIENTAL THOUGHT

An Introduction to the Philosophical
and Religious Thought of Asia

YONG CHOON KIM, Ph.D.

Department of Philosophy
University of Rhode Island
Kingston, Rhode Island

With a Foreword By

David H. Freeman, Ph.D.
Chairman
Department of Philosophy
University of Rhode Island
Kingston, Rhode Island

ROWMAN AND LITTLEFIELD
Totowa, New Jersey

published 1981 in Library edition by Rowman and Littlefield,
81 Adams Drive, Totowa, New Jersey 07512

Library of Congress Cataloging in Publication Data

Kim, Yong Choon.
  Oriental thought.

  Reprint of the ed. published by Thomas, Spring-
field, Ill.
  Includes bibliographical references and index.
  1. Philosophy, Oriental.   2. Civilization,
Oriental.   I. Title.
[B121.K5   1981b]   291'.095   80-39672
ISBN 0-8476-6972-6

Printed in the United States of America

FOREWORD

Contact between East and West has shown that the boundary between Oriental and Western thought is indeed an artificial one. Dr. Kim's book provides an excellent introduction to the world of the East. Within a very few pages Dr. Kim has captured the essence of Indian, Chinese, Japanese, and Korean thought. His treatment is sympathetic to all, but his critical insights and comparisons make this short book an example of oriental thought at its best. The reader who knows little will learn much, and the reader who already knows much, will learn more.

David H. Freeman

PREFACE

Cultural contact between the East and the West has increased rapidly in recent decades. Knowledge of the ideas and beliefs of other peoples is essential for the civilized man. In recent years the West has become more curious about Eastern thought, and has directed more attention to it.

In any human society thought is the essence of culture, and culture is the expression of the quality of thought. Oriental thought has its depth, breadth, and height like Western thought. The history of Oriental thought spans over three thousand years. Its long development involved many different thinkers and many complex systems.

One of the important characteristics of Oriental thinking, especially in the traditional East is that philosophy and religion often share common issues and a common area of concern. The ultimate concern of the Oriental mind in general has been not merely a rational understanding of God, Reality, or Truth, but intuitive, personal, ethical, or existential understanding of self and Reality. Often the climax of Oriental thought is an existential or intuitive encounter with the so-called Reality. Hence, a mystical element is strong in Oriental thought.

My approach in this book has been analytical, comparative, and critical. Since most Western readers are familar with Judeo-Christian thought, a comparison between Judeo-Christian thought and Oriental thought may be a good way of introducing Oriental thought.

There is an interesting contrast between Judeo-Christian thought and Oriental thought as a whole. While Judeo-Christian thought is basically theistic, Oriental thought by and large, except certain segments of Hinduism, is characterized as humanistic. While the center of Judeo-Christian thought is God, that of Oriental thought is man. While Judeo-Christian thought begins and ends with God, Oriental thought begins and ends with man.

Jews and Christians claim the historically witnessed revelation from God as their ultimate basis of truth, while Oriental philosophers in general do not claim such a revelation. Perhaps, an exception in Oriental systems is to be found in Hinduism which claims to have a revealed truth, however, without any claim to historical evidence. The divine revelation in history is the source of authority for Jews and Christians, while the mystical intuition of the human mind is the source of authority for Oriental thought. Hence, Oriental thought is speculative, subjectivistic in nature, while Judeo-Christian thought is avowedly based on the objective reality of revealed truth.

Buddhism, Confucianism, Taoism, and Ch'ondogyo represent the typical Oriental humanism, a man-centered philosophy. Judeo-Christian philosophy is a definite theism, a God-centered philosophy in which Yahweh (Jehovah) is the only true God, who is the Creator and the Ruler of the universe and man. This situation is different in Oriental thought on the whole, even though some Oriental religions recognize the existence of God.

Hinduism is theistic but the Hindu notion of God is confusing and irrational, for within its concept of God, polytheism, pantheism, and monotheism coexist. Brahman is the unique idea of a deity in Hinduism. Brahman is beyond everything and impersonal, and therefore Brahman is It, yet Brahman is all things, personal, and therefore Brahman is He. This notion appears to many to be confusing and illogical. The Shinto idea of God is polytheistic like that of Hinduism. Both the Hindu and Shinto notions of god are highly mythological. Buddhism recognizes the existence of many gods, but they are neither ultimate nor absolute. Buddha, which is the enlightened man, is the ultimate and absolute reality according to Buddhism. Some sectarian Buddhists worship deified Buddhas such as Amida Buddha. On the whole, however, Buddhists rely on their own strength for salvation, and in the final analysis they believe in themselves. There is no god to believe according to most Buddhists, especially Zen Buddhists, and therefore, Buddhism is sometimes called an atheism.

Confucianism recognizes the existence of "Heaven." But often this term "Heaven" has been used in Confucianism ambiguously without a clear definition. It is sometimes recognized as a Supreme Being, who has a controlling power over the fate of men, and sometimes re-garded as an impersonal cosmic power. It is not like the Judeo-Christian God who has intimate love and concern for men, who comes into personal fellowship and communion with men, who redeems men by grace, and who is the purposive Creator and Ruler of men and the universe in every detail.

The Taoist notion of *Tao* as the eternal, ultimate, and absolute reality of the universe is utterly impersonal; *Tao* has no personal relation with men. There is no personal love and grace of God for men in Taoism, while in Judeo-Christian thought the love, mercy, grace, holiness, and justice of God are central. In a similar way, the notion of *Li* in Neo-Confucianism as the ultimate principle of the universe is a cold, abstract idea which has no redemptive grace for men. The Ch'ondogyo notion of "Heaven" or God is similar to the impersonal Brahman or the Taoist notion of *Tao* and at times the Confucian idea of "Heaven."

The concept of the world is also a significant point of contrast between Judeo-Christian thought and Oriental thought. The world in Judeo-Christian thought is definitely the creation of God which He rules with a clear purpose and omnipotent will. In Judeo- Christian philosophy history is linear, has a definite beginning and end, and has a goal, as it is controlled by the personal God. But in Oriental thought as represented by Hinduism and Buddhism the world and history are cyclic, and in them there is no purpose and no real mean-ing. This world is viewed by Hinduism and Buddhism as *samsara,* reincarnation or transfiguration of soul, which is the continual cycle of rebirth and redeath. It is also viewed as *maya,* illusion or unreality. This is a pessimistic view of the world. In Confucianism, Taoism, and Shinto also, we find no meaningful eschatology that can answer the eternal and ultimate destiny of man and the world, although they vaguely imagine and project a peaceful world through man's col-lective self-effort.

The concept of man is another important aspect of contrast be-tween Eastern and Judeo-Christian thought. Man in Judeo-Christian philosophy is the image of God, a rational, moral, and religious creature. Man is finite and is never identified with God. His original nature was good and sinless. But his nature became depraved after the Fall of Adam, the disobedience of man. In contrast to this view, Hinduism claims that the real self of man is *Atman,* which is identical with *Brahman* which is God. Thus, according to Hinduism the very nature of man is divine. Such a deification of man is a great sin in Judeo-Christian thought.

Buddhism claims that man does not have a real, eternal, substantial soul or self. Man's goal is to reach Nirvana which is the extinction of ego, the state of nothingness. This notion of Nirvana appears to many to be abstract and nihilistic, while the Christian idea of the Kingdom of God or eternal life is a concrete reality.

Confucianism and Taoism do not provide any clear and uniform definition of the nature of man. Some Confucians disputed among themselves whether man's original nature is good or evil. Their notions were speculative and subjective, while the Judeo-Christian view is based on divine revelation which provides a clear answer to the origin and the nature of man. Taoism has the notion of emanation regarding the origin of man and the world, while Jews and Christians hold the concept of creation.

While Judeo-Christian thought provides a definite explanation of the origin and nature of sin as the disobedience of man to God's law, most Oriental philosophies and religions do not provide such an explanation. Sin in Hinduism and Buddhism is ignorance. In Confucianism, Taoism, and Shinto, the notion of sin is vague and ambiguous.

Because of the different notions of God, man, and sin, the notions of salvation are different in Judeo-Christian thought than in Oriental thought. The concept of redemption through the Messiah is unique in Judeo-Christian thought. Such an idea is absent in most Oriental religions. While Judeo-Christian thought maintains the idea of salvation by God's grace, most Asian religions do not contain such an idea. Most Eastern religions believe that salvation is achieved through man's self-effort. While the motive of salvation in Judeo-Christian thought is divine love, that of most Eastern religions is man's realization of his own inadequacy and determination to overcome it. Thus, Judeo-Christian thought is essentially theistic, and begins and ends with God's sovereign grace and will, while Oriental thought is basically humanistic, and begins and ends with man's subjective speculation and effort.

This book deals with the major areas of Oriental thought: Hinduism and Buddhism in India; Confucianism, Taoism, and Neo-Confucianism in China; Shamanism, Buddhism, Confucianism, and Ch'ondogyo in Korea; Shinto and Buddhism in Japan. It is not intended as a detailed study of Oriental thought, but rather as a concise and comprehensive presentation of the most important aspects of Oriental thought.

I have been planning to write such a book for several years. As a teacher of Oriental thought, I have long recognized the need for a concise introductory textbook. The purpose of this book is to provide a basic introduction to the philosophical and religious ideas of the East. The book is intended as a basic text for such courses as Oriental Philosophy, Eastern Religions, World Religions, Comparative Religion, and Comparative Thought. It can also be used in Philosophy of Religion, Introduction to Religion, Introduction to Philosophy, and Asian Culture. It may be used with a few anthologies that are already available.

This book should be useful to anyone who begins the study of Oriental Philosophy or Eastern Religions, for it has been written with introductory level students in mind. However, the general reader who is interested in Oriental thought and culture should also find it readable and informative.

I wish to thank the following persons to whom I am greatly indebted for the fruition of this work: Dr. David Freeman, Chairman of the Philosophy Department at the University of Rhode Island, whose encouragement and help were a vital source of strength for the success of this work; Dr. Raymond Haskell who kindly rendered editoral help; and my wife, Chung Ja who patiently rendered moral support for a long period of time.

YONG CHOON KIM

CONTENTS

ORIENTAL THOUGHT

An Introduction to the Philosophical and Religious Thought of Asia

PART ONE

INDIAN THOUGHT

INDIAN THOUGHT HAS A LONG AND COMPLEX DEVELOPMENT. IT IS DIFFICULT TO GIVE AN EXACT HISTORICAL ACCOUNT OF THE DEVELOPMENT OF INDIAN THOUGHT AND ITS MANY WRITINGS, ESPECIALLY OF ITS EARLY STAGE. THERE IS, IN FACT, NO SINGLE PHILOSOPHY OR RELIGION IN INDIA, BUT MANY DIFFERENT KINDS, ALTHOUGH HINDUISM, WITH ITS COMPLEX BRANCHES, REPRESENTS THE MAJOR RELIGION IN INDIA.

THE INDIAN MIND IS CHARACTERIZED BY ITS EMPHASIS ON INWARD REALITY, INNER BEAUTY AND SPIRITUAL CULTURE. THUS, PHILOSOPHY AND RELIGION ARE INSEPARABLY RELATED IN THE INDIAN MIND. PHILOSOPHY IN INDIA IS NO MORE THAN THE SPIRITUAL UNDERSTANDING OF THE RELIGIOUS AND PHILOSOPHICAL CONCERNS ABOUT THE ULTIMATE REALITY. THE TRANS-TEMPORAL SEARCH FOR THE ULTIMATE ANSWER FOR LIFE WAS AN IMPORTANT ELEMENT IN THE INDIAN MIND. THUS, IT MAY BE STATED THAT IDEALISM IS A STRONG ELEMENT IN INDIAN PHILOSOPHY. REALITY IS CONCEIVED AS ULTIMATELY SPIRITUAL AND NOT MATERIAL. AND REALITY IS CONCEIVED AS ULTIMATELY ONE.

INDIAN PHILOSOPHY IS ALSO CHARACTERIZED BY ITS EMPHASIS ON INTUITION RATHER THAN ON REASON. INDIAN PHILOSOPHY USES REASON, BUT IT REGARDS INTUITION AS THE ULTIMATE GUIDE TO REALIZING THE TRUTH.

CHAPTER I

 **HINDUISM**

THE DEVELOPMENT OF HINDUISM

THE HINDUS call their religion eternal law or eternal truth. Hinduism is called also a-historical or non-historical religion, for it is said that there is no historical beginning and no human author. Although it is true that there is no single founder of Hinduism, it seems to be an oversimplification to assume that there was no beginning for Hinduism. There was a sort of primitive stage at the beginning point of early Hinduism, in which a writing system was unknown. Thus, this may be called the a-historical stage or very primitive pre-historical stage of Hinduism. Nevertheless, there is the generally known historical development of Hinduism which may be divided into four major periods.[1]

First is the Vedic Period, which is approximately 2500 to 600 B.C. During this period the Aryans invaded India from Central Asia and brought the new and more advanced civilization. This was the period in which the primitive elements of religious thought abounded, and yet major philosophical ideas also began to develop in the Upanishads.

The writings of this period consist of the four Vedas, which are Rig-Veda, Yajur-Veda, Sama-Veda, and Atharva-Veda. Each of the four Vedas has four parts, known as Mantras, Brahmanas, Aranyakas, and Upanishads. The Mantras are hymns; they constitute the beginning of Indian philosophy. There is a progressive movement in them from polytheism of the early Vedas, through monotheism, to suggestions of monism. They paved the way for the monistic philosophy of the Upanishads.

The Brahmanas, which interpret Brahman, are primarily religious documents including ritualistic ideas and sacrificial rules. The Aranyakas and the Upanishads are the concluding parts of the Brahmanas. The Aranyakas (forest-teaching) encourage meditation for those who live in the forest, which is an ideal stage following the stage of a householder. The Upanishads are primarily the works of philosophers. Upanishads mean that pupils sat near the teacher to learn the truth. There is a strong tendency to spiritual monism in them, in which the central characteristics of Indian philosophy have developed, and in which intuition rather than reason is recognized as the true guide to ultimate truth.

The second period of Indian philosophical development is the Epic Period, approximately 500 B.C. to 200 A.D. In this period the philosophical ideas were expressed indirectly through the great epics like the Mahabharata. In this period, Buddhism and Jainism also developed. The Bhagavad-Gita, which is part of the Mahabharata, is one of the most important literatures that belong to this age.

The third period is the Sutra Period, dated approximately from the Fourth Century B.C. to the Fifth Century A.D. The systematic treatises of the various schools developed in this period. The Samkhya system of evolutionary dualism, the Yoga system of disciplined meditation, and the Vedanta system of largely monistic philosophy are chief parts of the Sutras.

The fourth period is called the Scholastic or Commentary Period, dated from about the Sixth Century A.D. to the modern age. In this period commentaries were written upon the Sutras. Among the great philosophers of this period, Samkara, Ramanuja, and Madhava are famous; Samkara's commentary on the Sutra of the Vedanta system is most important.

Indian philosophy had a serious decline approximately in the seventeenth century when outside powers began to dominate India. However, since the nineteenth century there has been a sort of revival and reform movement in Hinduism through some outstanding thinkers such as Ramakrishna, Sri Aurobindo, and Radhakrishnan. One of the main reasons for such a movement is that during the last century there was an increasing exchange of ideas between India and the West. Radhakrishnan, the former President of India, was one of the greatest thinkers; he attempted to synthesize the Eastern thought with the Western thought.

IDEAS OF GOD

The Hindu ideas of God are as complex as Hinduism itself. Within the Hindu ideas of God almost all sorts of categories exist. The Hindu ideas of God may be defined in terms of polytheism, pantheism, monotheism, and monism.

Polytheism

In contrast to the absolute monotheism of the major Western religions represented by Judaism, Christianity, and Islam, Hinduism is characterized by polytheism and pantheism. There are many gods and goddesses whom the Hindus worship. The Hindu polytheism is most clearly seen in the hymns of the Rig-Veda.[2]

In the history of Indian ideas of God, a naturalistic polytheism occupies the early stage. The Vedic gods were identified with certain forces of nature, and they were gradually promoted to moral and superhuman beings. The early seers of the Vedic hymns saw the things of nature with such intensity of imagination that the things became suffused with souls. The Indian mind at this stage belonged to primitive polytheism, making gods in the image of man himself.

Radhakrishnan states that the ideas of the Rig-Veda are important because they represent the earliest stages of Indian philosophical thought in India, and because they are the source of the later practices and philosophies of India.[3]

Among the Vedic pantheon only several need to be mentioned. Indra is the god of thunderstorm, the atmospheric phenomena, and of the blue sky, but gradually he became the ruler of all the world and all creatures. Agni is the god of fire who consumes the sacrifice. He is the mediator between gods and men. Vishnu is the all-pervader in whom abide all creatures. Varuna is chief of the gods of the natural and moral order. He is regarded as the highest ethical creation of the Vedic Indians. He is the guardian of the cosmic law. Varuna is the ruler of man, nature, and the whole universe. In the case of Varuna there is a tendency toward monotheism. "Attributes moral and spiritual, such as justice, beneficence, righteousness, and even pity were ascribed to him."[4]

On the whole, the world of the Vedas is the world of mythology and subjective fantasy.[5] In the Vedas there are strange utterances of incantations, spells, charms, witchcraft, hymns to inanimate things, devils, and demons to insure safe birth, to expel diseases, etc. They are the main theme of the Atharva Veda. Thus, Radhakrishnan states, "The religion of the Atharva-Veda is that of the primitive man, to whom the world is full of shapeless ghosts and spirits of death."[6]

Later, Brahmanism invented an artificial "trinity" of gods in Hinduism, the idea of one God in three forms: Brahma, the creator; Vishnu, the preserver; and Shiva, the destroyer. But most Hindus are worshipers of either Vishnu or Shiva, each of which is regarded by their worshipers as the supreme god.

Pantheistic Monism and Monotheism

In the *Upanishads* which are the concluding parts of the Vedas we find monotheism and monism of Hinduism. Many of the Upanishads belong to the eighth and seventh centuries B.C. The authors of the Upanishads are unknown. There is a strong and intensive search for the ultimate reality in the Upanishads. The ultimate concern for the ultimate reality, which is the source and ground of all existences and all movements, is very strongly emphasized in the Upanishads.

The ultimate reality which is at the heart of the universe and which embraces all beings is called *Brahman*. All gods and all beings are simply the manifestations of one ultimate being, Brahman. "He (Brahman) is Brahma, he is Shiva, he is Indra, he is the supreme, the changeless reality. He is Vishnu, he is the primal energy . . . ."[7] Thus, the Hindu idea of god here is clearly expressed as pantheistic monotheism or monism. Brahman is one and yet many. Brahman, the eternal and imperishable One is the manifold Brahman, for all gods and all beings pass into that imperishable. Brahman is the priest god (Agni) and the warrior god (Indra).[8] So the all is centered on the One and identified totally with the One. This is, therefore, a pantheistic monism.

Brahman as the ultimate reality and as the essence of all things in the universe is the foundational concept in the Hindu metaphysics. Brahman in itself as beyond manifestation is regarded as impersonal, indescribable, and undefinable. It is pure absolute and *neti neti* (not this, not that), which means that it is beyond identification. It is wholly other and totally transcendent reality.

In the *Bhagavad-Gita* (Song of the Lord), which is a part of the Mahabharata, an epic of about the sixth century B.C., we find a strong trend toward theism in contrast to the Upanishads in which the impersonal aspect of Brahman as absolute reality was emphasized. In the *Gita,* God is transcendental and yet personal. He creates the world by his nature. The *Gita* stresses the redeeming role of Vishnu. Krishna, an incarnation of God into human form, represents the Vishnu aspect of the ultimate being.[9]

In these developments of the Hindu ideas of gods, we may be able to sense a subjective projection of human mind, for it seems apparent that the transition from chaotic polytheism of the Vedas to a unifying idea of pantheistic monism in the Upanishads, and then from the impersonal idea of God to the more personal idea of God in the Gita, is the projection of man's imagination to satisfy his religious and philosophical desires.

WORLD AND REINCARNATION

Dharma

It is the *Dharma* by which the whole universe is controlled and operated. Dharma means *law* or *truth.* Nothing is outside its realm of rule. All existences—man, world, and gods—are under the Dharma, which is the supreme regulatory principle of the universe.

Within the framework of Dharma, the most important categories that govern the world and man are *samsara, karma,* and *moksha.*

Samsara

Samsara may be translated as reincarnation, rebirth, or transmigration of soul. This world is generally regarded as the world of samsara, but any part of the universe where any type of existence remains without the final liberation (moksha) may be called a part of the world of samsara. Samsara is a supreme mark of unreality according to Hinduism, for it is essentially transient, changing, painful, and sorrowful. It signifies constant repetition of pains, sorrows of life, and death. Life which has constant recurrence of death is obviously no real life.

Reincarnation repeats again and again that all beings should work out another karma until they reach *moksha* (liberation). The doctrine of reincarnation is accepted by all philosophical schools of Hinduism as a self-evident fact of existence.[10] Zaehner states:

> This doctrine itself presupposes the further doctrine that the condition into which the individual soul is reborn is itself the result of good or bad actions performed in former lives; and these actions and the modifications they produce in the myriad sum total of ever-reincarnating souls from eternity without beginning to eternity without end themselves constitute the stuff of the moral as distinct from the natural universe. Yet no hard and fast distinction can be made between the two, for the same ineluctable law of cause and effect rules both. This is the law of *karma* ('action'), the law according to which any action whatsoever is the effect of a cause and is in its turn the cause of an effect. The whole process goes by the name of *samsara,* the 'course' or 'revolution' to which all phenomenal existence is subject, and which is itself subject to and conditioned by an endless causal past, the *dharma* of the universe.[11]

Time

To the Dharma (law) of the universe and reincarnation there is neither beginning nor end, neither for the universe nor for the individual soul. Hindu philosophy assumes that the universe is governed by cyclic time. According to Zaehner, "Time is a revolving wheel returning ever again to the point from which it started, and in it there can be neither purpose nor salvation.[12] This is a sort of pessimistic attitude regarding this world and life. It is also a sort of meaningless determinism. Such a concept of cyclic time is exactly opposite to the Judeo-Christian concept of time and history as linear, in which there is a definite starting point and orderly progress and final point according to the exact purpose and plan of the sovereign God, who is both the Creator and Judge of the world.

Origin of the World

In so far as the origin of the world is concerned, there is no one single theory, but several confusing theories in Hinduism. The early Vedic thinkers thought of the origin and nature of the world mythologically. The following quotation from Radhakrishnan would show the mythological picture of the making of the world in Hinduism:

In the pluralistic stage the several gods, Varuna, Indra, Agni, Vishvakarman, were looked upon as the authors of the universe. The method of creation is differently conceived. Some gods are supposed to build the world as the carpenter builds a house. The question is raised as to how the tree or the wood out of which the work was built was obtained. At a later stage the answer is given that Brahman is the tree and the wood out of which heaven and earth are made. The conception of organic growth or development is also now and then suggested. Sometimes the gods are said to create the world by the power of sacrifice. This perhaps belongs to a later stage of Vedic thought.

When we get to the monotheistic level, the question arises as to whether God created the world out of His own nature without any pre-existent matter or through His power acting on eternally pre-existent matter. The former view takes us to the higher monistic conception, while the latter remains at the lower monotheistic level, and we have both views in the Vedic hymns.[13]

The Rig-Veda postulates water as the sole primeval matter from which others developed. Later Indian thinkers postulate five basic elements as the essential constitution of the world. Concerning the question whether the existence or being sprang from the non-existent or non-being, the Hindu answer is that distinct being comes from non-distinct being.

A distinct concept of the creation of the world in Hindu philosophy is that the gods were the agents of creation, while the material world out of which the world is made is the body of the great Purusha. The act of creation is a sacrifice in which Purusha is the victim.[14]

In the *Upanishads* we find a different account of the origin of the world. The origin of all things is now interpreted in terms of one absolute ground of the universe, Brahman, which is the uncaused great cause.[15] The transcendent reality, Brahman, is the sole and the whole explanation of the world, its material and efficient cause. Brahman, the everlasting one, is the sole source of life in all that lives. This Brahman is also called the ultimate ground of being.[16] There is a very interesting similarity here between the term, God as the "Ground of Being" used by the famous Protestant philosopher-theologian of the twentieth century, Paul Tillich, and the term, Brahman as the "ultimate ground of being" used by the foremost Indian philosopher of this century, Radhakrishnan.

The monistic view of the origin of the universe in the Upanishads is again different from the *Samkhya* dualism of the later period (c. the Third Century A.D.) which is an evolutionary theory of the universe. According to the Samkhya, there are two fundamental categories: Purusha, which is the subject or source of spirituality, and Prakriti which is the object or source of the material universe. Prakriti (nature) is the basis of all objective existence, physical and psychical, and it is the source of the world of becoming. But the evolution of unconscious Prakriti takes place only through the presence of conscious Purusha.[17]

On the whole, the Hindu concept of the creation of the world is quite different from the Judeo-Christian concept of the creation, for the former is complex and confused to a great extent, and it is a mixture of creation and evolution. The latter presents a clear, simple, and definitive account of creation by one sovereign and personal God by His Word. There is no confusing and contradictory account of creation in the Bible of Jews and Christians, while such confusing and contradictory ideas of the origin of the world are abundant in the Hindu writings.

Maya

Concerning the nature of the world, a dualistic Hindu would say that the natural world is as real as God, while a non-dualistic Hindu would say that the world as it now appears to us is *maya,* "illusion." Although *maya* in Rig-Veda often means occult and mysterious power, and it has various meanings in different schools of Hinduism, the significant and primary philosophical meaning of it in the Vedanta is "illusion."

The Hindus claim that this world has a kind of qualified or provisional reality. The non-dualist Hindu claims that one must see all things as one reality, Brahman. This perception is called wisdom in the monistic Hinduism, which in effect produces *moksha.* At this point, there seems to be a grave contradiction in Hindu thought. If the wisdom means to see all things, even this world, as one absolute reality, Brahman, why should man search for *moksha* from the world of samsara, to begin with? Logically, this pantheistic monism has a terrible defect, because, if all things are part of Brahman, the escape from samsara would be utterly unnecessary and meaningless.

Karma

The *samsara* is governed by *karma*. *Karma* may be translated as law of cause and effect, work, deed, or action. There is no samsara without karma. Reincarnation takes place because there is a causing factor. This idea of karma is the basis of the caste system in Hindu society. Its function as an ethical principle in society is also very powerful, as it prohibits every Hindu from performing any bad karma. Perhaps, this is a more effective way of controlling large Indian masses than any other external police power could. Thus, we may safely state that the law of karma is invisible yet real "police" in each individual life in Hindu society. The idea and role of karma is practically the same in Buddhist society as in Hindu society, since Buddhism adopted the idea of karma from Hinduism.

We cannot be sure whether the ideas of karma and samsara were invented by Indian philosophers deliberately to insure the orderly existence and operation of society, or that they were conceived simply to explain the situation that already existed in Indian society. Radhakrishnan states the basic function of karma as follows:

> The law of karma is the counter-part in the moral world of the physical law of uniformity. It is the law of the conservation of moral energy. . . . According to the principle of karma there is nothing uncertain or capricious in the moral world. We reap what we sow. The good seed brings a harvest of good, the evil of evil.[18]

In the law of karma we find that the great emphasis is placed upon an individual's responsibility for his actions. A man's present state of life is determined by his past karma, and his future destiny will be determined by his present karma, whether it is good or bad. "A man becomes good by good deeds and bad by bad deeds."[19] Chandogya Upanishad states: "Man is a creature of will. According as he believes in this world, so will he be when he is departed."[20] It states again, "Whatever world he covets by his mind, and whatever objects he wishes, for the man of pure mind, he gains those worlds and those objects."[21] Hence, because of the karma, the wheel of samsara turns with birth and death, beginningless and endless. All beings and existences, such as men, gods, animals, and plants, are embraced by this universal norm of karma.

The doctrine of karma places moral responsibility upon an individual for his deeds, and thus it gives hope for improvement of his lot in the future. But it seems to have a tremendous weakness in its dogmatic assertion of one's state in the present life as the result of one's apparently unknown past existence.

The dogmatic and categorical placement of the members of Hindu society within the framework of caste system, some highest, some high, some low, and others lowest, just simply because of birth in a certain caste, seems to be a terribly unjust and unreasonable way of treating persons in the modern world in which democratic spirit prevails. Although there is a democratic change taking place in the present Indian society due to the influence of Western democracy, the change is slow. Yet vast masses of people live under the shadow of the traditional caste system, which is divided into Brahmins (priests), Kshatriyas (nobles and warriors), Vaisyas (peasants and artisans), and Shudras (servants). Below these castes, there has been the so-called "untouchables," who are also called the "outcastes," to whom Gandhi gave a new name, *Harijans,* which means "God's people."

Why should some remain as garbage collectors or toilet cleaners for their entire lives just because they are born into families of the untouchables? Such undemocratic and discriminatory practices seem to be ugly ills in Indian society. Gandhi and other Indian leaders tried to correct the ills of the caste system to some extent, but it seems that they did not try hard enough. Although the Indian government abolished the caste system by law in principle, it may stay a long time as a practice among the Indian masses. It is simply too deeply rooted in the culture and hearts of Indian people and in their so-called sacred writings.

SELF AND REALIZATION

Moksha

Moksha means spiritual liberation. It is the goal of all beings. According to Hinduism it is possible for all beings to attain final spiritual liberation from the bondage of this world of samsara. All forms of religious and philosophical search in India have one ultimate goal, which is moksha. Moksha as the supreme liberation signifies that the bondage of unreal life, characterized by old age, sickness, death, sorrow, fear, and all kinds of pain, is completely and finally broken, and real life of absolute joy and peace takes its place. Moksha is an aspect of dharma, the universal law, which governs all beings.

The search for gods in the Hindu religious philosophy has been in a sense a search for moksha, although often the different ideas of god seem confusing and contradictory. It is often said that the Indian mind in general did not search for mere rational or intellectual understanding of life but for the realization of self, which is, in effect, moksha. Many Hindus place higher value on the inner spiritual cultivation of self than on material wealth and bodily pleasure. Perhaps, that is why there are many naked ascetics wandering all over India with dust over their bodies. In India these ascetics are often regarded as holy men who are more highly respected than in any other part of the world, for they search not for wealth and power in the world, but for eternal liberation and union with God, which is the realization of self, according to Hinduism.

Brahman-Atman

In the primitive religion of the Vedas, it was primarily through worship of gods in the forms of hymns, prayers, and sacrifices that the Hindus aimed at the realization of self. But later in the Upanishads, we find the concept of self and its realization expressed in terms of complete union of individual self with universal self. In a practical term it may be called the union of man and God. Here, at this stage of Hinduism, we find the development of a radical monism. In the Upanishads God is both transcendent and immanent. It is an indescribable and indefinable Absolute in itself, and yet it is within each individual self. *Brahman* is wholly other in itself as beyond manifestation and somewhat impersonal "It," yet it is also personal God, "He" in its manifestation. This Brahman, the cosmic Self is, according to the Upanishads, none other than *Atman,* the innermost self or soul of each individual man.

Such an immanent idea of God lies in contrast to the wholly transcendent idea of God in the Rig-Veda. In the Upanishads, the subjective and the objective, the Brahman and the Atman, the cosmic and the psychical principles, are identical. Brahman is Atman.[22] This expression characterizes the Hindu view of reality as a pantheistic monism as well as an ontological mysticism.

The Upanishadic Hinduism seeks this union of God and man as the ultimate goal of life. The point of union of Brahman and Atman is the point of moksha, the liberation from samsara and karma. But there seems to be a very grave inherent contradiction in this most fundamental concept of Hinduism. If man's essential self, Atman, is God, Brahman, why is there need to seek the union of man and God, to begin with? Of course, the Hindus may interpret that since the oneness of Brahman and Atman is the goal to seek to realize, it is not the present reality for souls in samsara. But often the Hindu literatures identify Brahman and Atman as if they are the present reality in this world.[23]

It is true, however, in the Hindu philosophy that self-realization is the supreme goal. If one realizes the universal Self in him, there is no point to worship or fear gods. Thus, the union of man and God in the Upanishads makes the worship of gods in the Vedas void and practically meaningless. The state of union of Brahman and Atman is expressed in terms of *tat tvam asi* (That thou art).[24] Such a radical identification of God and man characterizes Hinduism as mysticism. The ultimate reality and the absolute truth is within man, according to Hindu mysticism. This perspective of reality indicates also that Hinduism is highly subjective philosophy and religion since there is no substantial objective evidence to verify the Hindu thesis of the identification of Brahman-Atman here. The subjectivism of the Upanishads seems to be the central character of Hindu philosophy.

The concept of the union of Brahman-Atman is the heart of the Vedanta philosophy, which is a system of Hindu philosophy with its basis in the Upanishads. Vedanta represents the central aspect of Hinduism. The Vedanta school emphasizes the non-duality or monism of divine-human relationship. To realize one's self to be identical with Brahman is the supreme wisdom and liberation itself, according to Hinduism.

Hinduism claims that to see things with discriminatory and dualistic eyes is the supreme mark of ignorance which causes desire and then repeated rebirth and death. Nikhilananda asserts as follows:

For if a person has realized himself to be Brahman, infinite and all-pervading, and if he sees himself in the universe and the universe in himself, he cannot desire anything. What can he desire who has found the fulfillment of all desires in the self? The knowledge that the self is the desireless Brahman is liberation.

This is the Vedantic conception of immortality, an immortality not to be attained in heaven, but here on earth in this very body through the knowledge of the immortal nature of the self. About the enlightened person the Upanishads say: "Having always been free, he realizes his freedom." "If a person is able to attain knowledge in this very life, then this knowledge is real for him; if he does not attain knowledge in this very life, then a great destruction awaits him."[25]

The above statement of Swami Nikhilananda seems to be a naive idealism. How many would there be in the world who cannot desire anything? Furthermore, if a person has been always free, why does he need to realize his freedom? If a person is free, does he need to know that he is free? If a person has always been free, then the very words, "bondage" or "reincarnation," which the Hindus use, seem to be meaningless. If the nature of a person is immortal, the word, "attaining" the immortality is needless and meaningless.

Anyhow, the Upanishadic Hinduism always emphasizes that man only needs to know his Atman, which is identical with Brahman. Then, one would transcend his desires, which cause the bondage of reincarnation. Concerning the self-knowledge, Swami Nikhilanada states:

> The attainment of self-knowledge is not a static condition beyond which the soul cannot move. This knowledge really indicates the soul's entrance into a new realm of consciousness. By his life and action, a free soul demonstrates the reality of Brahman, the divinity of man, and the oneness of existence.[26]

Such a statement of a Hindu thinker manifestedly demonstrates the radically pantheistic monism as a fundamental characteristic of the Hindu philosophy of man. We find here a clear evidence of the deification of man, which would be a supreme mark of sin in the Judeo-Christian tradition. In sharp contrast with the Hindu concept of human self as identical with the divine self, Christianity maintains the clear cut and absolute distinction between the Creator-God and man, the creature. In Christianity man is never more than the image of God. Man is neither God nor can he become God in Judeo-Christian tradition.

Concerning the destiny of a knower of the self after death, the monistic Hinduism maintains that he who is without desires is not embodied again. Being Brahman, he merges in Brahman. Concerning the destiny of the soul of the knower of Atman, Nikhilananda states as follows:

> Just as the lifeless slough of a snake is cast off, and lies on an anthill, so does his body lie; his soul shines as Brahman. As milk poured into milk becomes one with the milk, as water poured into water becomes one with water, as oil poured into oil becomes one with the oil, so the illumined soul absorbed in Brahman becomes one with Brahman. A free soul, however, out of compassion for mankind, may of his own free will again assume a human body and work for the welfare of mankind.
>
> Once his ignorance is destroyed, a man enters into the realm of light, freedom, knowledge, and reality and never comes back to the world of darkness, bondage, ignorance, and illusion. Once the butterfly has emerged from the chrysalis, it no more crawls on the earth, but flits flower to flower, bathed in the light of the sun.
>
> Such is the ultimate destiny of the human soul.[27]

Again in the above statement the question arises: If the human soul is divine in its essence, what has knowledge or ignorance to do with change of the constitutional essence of man? To know that man's soul is divine or to realize that Brahman is within man would imply that man is ontologically eternal God prior to the event of knowledge. Hence, there is no good logical rationality in the concept of Brahman-Atman. If it is to become entirely logical, Hinduism should have stated that man is Brahman even before the realization, and therefore, man is immortal, and he would not need to be absorbed in Brahman. If man is Brahman, should he not be a knower in the first place? To state it conversely, if man is ignorant, he could not be Brahman. But to deny the Brahmanhood of man would be to reject the pantheistic monism of Hindu philosophy. Thus, this is the most critical weakness in the Vedanta concept of the self and its realization.

Yogas

Hinduism suggests various methods of securing paths to realization; they are called Four Paths to the goal. The word *yoga* may be defined as a method of training or disciplining which leads to self-realization or the union of man and God. It is the spiritual exercise of meditation. The basic aim is to achieve the union of man's soul with God, who is hidden deep in the darkest part of our being. To discover the infinite ocean of the force of life is the purpose of the Hindu yoga concentration.

> And since all the Indian spiritual exercises are devoted seriously to this practical aim—not to a merely fanciful contemplation or discussion of lofty and profound ideas—they may well be regarded as representing one of the most realistic, matter-of-fact, practical-minded systems of thought and training ever set up by the human mind. How to come to Brahman and remain in touch with it; how to become divine while still on earth-transformed, reborn adamantine while on the earthly plane; that is the quest that has inspired and deified the spirit of man in India through the ages.[28]

Hinduism provides the four different paths for the goal of realization. What is the reason for the four rather than just one path? Well, the Hindus explain that there are different starting points for the basically four different types of people in the world. Some are essentially active, some are basically emotional, some are intellectual in temperament, and others are empirical in their basic approach. Thus, there are the four yogas for those four different kinds of persons. Often these yogas are practiced together inclusively by many Hindus.

Karma Yoga

The first type is *karma-yoga,* which means yoga of work. By performing moral duties and good actions, one achieves the goal of self-realization. Work performed as a spiritual discipline is a predominant topic of the Bhagavad-Gita. The secrets of karma yoga are to be free from selfish motive for the fruit of action, attachment, the desire to possess, and anger, etc. It is service for God and for men, through which one attains purification of the mind and realization of the truth.[29]

Bhakti Yoga

The second type is *bhakti-yoga,* which is path of love. This yoga is basically designed for persons who consider love as chief guide and approach to God. Love is indeed the most common and universal aspect of human life. Love is the most pervasive and powerful element in life, and it is more powerful than reason, which is often cold. It also alienates men in the course of endless arguments. Thus, many people prefer to cling to or resort to love as the bosom of life and the refuge of comfort. As love grows, one comes to true relationship with reality in life. In the bhakti-yoga the basic requirement is to love God dearly. In the deepest dimension of love, all ulterior reason and selfish motives disappear, and the union of God and man is realized, according to the Hindu thought. Adoring and worshiping God in complete love and calling his name repeatedly in prayer and hymn are the modes of bhakti-yoga as the path to salvation in Hinduism. This yoga is greatly emphasized in the Bhagavad-Gita. Often this yoga leads to mysticism in Hinduism.

Jnana Yoga

The third type of path is called *jnana-yoga,* the way of knowledge. It is designed for basically intellectually inclined persons who may realize the union of man's soul with God through knowledge. There are persons who are interested in the philosophical quest and search for the ultimate answer for the supreme concern of man and world. For such persons, jnana-yoga is the best approach to the goal.

Jnana-yoga is much discussed in Vedanta, which is largely the system of non-dualism.[30] It is the discipline of philosophical search by which knowledge of Brahman is attained. To the non-dualists of Vedanta philosophy, the real knowledge is that Brahman alone is real; the phenomenal world is unreal; all beings are Brahman. To them jnana-yoga establishes the sole reality of Brahman. The ultimate oneness of the Godhead, all living beings, and the universe is especially emphasized by Samkara as the essential teaching of Vedanta as expounded in the Upanishads and the Bhagavad-Gita.[31]

To know the oneness of all things as grounded in one ultimate and absolute Brahman is the goal in jnana-yoga. Jnana-yoga emphasizes the study of Vedanta and intuitive knowledge. It emphasizes the control of the body and the senses, control of the mind, and complete concentration. It also emphasizes longing for freedom.[32] At the end, the student (yoga) must be able to utter "That thou art," which is the mystical expression of the complete oneness of individual self with the universal Self.

Raja Yoga

The fourth type is *raja-yoga,* which may be called the royal path or spiritual discipline. It is designed for persons who are basically empirical and psychological in bent. It is the path to the ultimate reality basically through psychological or spiritual exercise. Raja-yoga is discipline or technique of controlling mind to still it. Patanjali, the ancient Hindu philosopher, who systematized these disciplines in the *Yoga-sutras,* has defined yoga as "the restraining of the mind from taking various forms."[33] Raja-yoga is essentially the practice of meditation and concentration. "According to raja-yoga, the waves of the mind can be controlled by practice and non-attachment."[34]

> The mind of a yogi practising concentration is disturbed at the beginning by many distractions, as is the surface of a lake by waves. But through persistent practice of concentration these distractions become attentuated. Intense concentration on the nature of the self creates a powerful wave, which gradually swallows up, as it were, all other waves created by past impressions. Finally, by utter nonattachment and a supreme act of will, the last wave can be made to burst and the mind becomes free from all distractions. It acquires its natural state of purity and reflects the true nature of the inner spirit or soul.[35]

There are eight steps or "limbs" in raja-yoga:

1. Abstentions: from injury, lying, stealing, sensuality, and greed.

2. Observances: such as austerity, study of scriptures, contentment, purity of body and mind, and contemplation of God. The first two are moral preparations.

3. Posture: the yogi sits erect, holding his back, neck and head in a straight line, and resting the whole weight of the upper body on the ribs. With the chest out, the yogi can relax the body and begin to meditate.

4. The control of the breath: proper breathing is absolutely required for proper meditation.

5. Detaching: senses from their various objects.

6. Concentration: fixing attention on one single object.

7. Meditation: flow of thought toward the object.

8. Absorption: the final, climactic, and mystical state in which man's mind is completely absorbed in God.

The last two steps are tremendously important in raja-yoga. Meditation *(dhyana)* is the deepest level of the concentration of mind, in which the subject and object are in the process of being merged into one reality. That very moment of the perfect and complete union of knower and known is called *samadhi,* the ecstatic or mystical absorption. At this final moment, a Hindu would declare, "That art thou." This expression denotes that the individual self is identical with the universal Self.[36]

On the whole, the Hindu thought here is psychological and spiritual exercise. By concentration and meditation, the Hindus seek to achieve union with God, but this union seems to be very much the union in the human mind and therefore subjectivistic. When the Hindus arrive at the moment of psychological ectasy, they call it *moksha,* the liberation.

FOOTNOTES

[1]S. Radhakrishnan and C. A. Moore (Eds.): *A Source Book in Indian Philosophy* (Princeton: Princeton University Press, 1970), xvii.

[2]Radhakrishnan, *Indian Philosophy* (New York: MacMillan Co., 1956), Vol. I, p. 72.

[3]*Op. cit.,* p. 3.

[4]*Indian Philosophy,* Vol. I, p. 90.

[5]Cf. David H. Freeman, *A Philosophical Study of Religion* (Nutley, N.J.: The Craig Press, 1964), p. 46.

[6]*Indian Philosophy,* Vol. I, p. 119.

[7]*The Upanishads,* trans. by S. Prabhavananda and F. Manchester (New York: New American Library (Mentor), 1961), p. 115.

[8]R. C. Zaehner, *Hinduism* (London: Oxford University Press, 1969), p. 49.

[9]*A Source Book in Indian Philosophy,* p. 101.

[10]Zaehner, p. 4.

[11]*Ibid.*

[12]*Ibid.,* pp. 5 and 62.

[13]*Indian Philosophy,* Vol. I, pp. 99-100.

[14]*Ibid.,* p. 105.

[15]Swami Nikhilananda, *Hinduism* (New York: Harper, 1958), p. 52.

[16]*Indian Philosophy,* Vol. I, p. 183.

[17]*A Source Book in Indian Philosophy,* p. 424.

[18]*Indian Philosophy, Vol. I,* pp. 244-45.

[19]Brh., iii. 2. 13 in *Indian Philosophy,* Vol. I, p. 245.

[20]Chān., iii. 14. 1 in *Ibid.*

[21]Chān., iii. 1. 10 in *Ibid.*

[22]*Ibid.,* p. 169.

[23]*Ibid.,* pp. 169ff.

[24]*A Source Book in Indian Philosophy,* P. 38.

[25]Nikhilananda, p. 53.

[26]*Ibid.*

[27]*Ibid.,* p. 56.

[28]Heinrich Zimmer, *Philosophies of India* (New York: Pantheon Books, 1951), pp. 80-81.

[29]Nikhilananda, pp. 95ff.

[30]Besides Vedanta as the philosophy of non-dualism, there are two other interpretations of Vedanta as qualified non-dualism represented by Ramanuja and dualism represented by Madhva. See *ibid.,* p. 116.

[31]*Ibid.,* Samkara is also called Sankaracharya. He is a very important philosopher of the eighth century A.D.

[32]*Ibid.,* pp. 119-120.

[33]*Ibid.,* p. 129.

[34]*Ibid.,* p. 131.

[35]*Ibid.,* pp. 136-137.

[36]Cf. *Ibid.,* p. 139

 BUDDHISM

INTRODUCTION

BUDDHISM ORIGINATED in India within the religious and social context of Hinduism, almost as Christianity did within the context of Judaism in Palestine. Buddhism adopted many Hindu ideas but it also rejected many Hindu ideas. Here it is unlike Christianity for it inherited the central thought of Judaism as that of the Old Testament and interpreted it in the light of the New Testament centered in Jesus the Christ. Buddhism, for example, accepted the Hindu ideas of reincarnation (samsara) and law of cause and effect (karma), but it rejected the Hindu doctrines of the caste system, Brahman as the Ultimate Reality, and the substantiality of man's soul or self.

Buddha

Unlike Hinduism, which has no founder, Buddhism has a historical founder known as Gautama Buddha, who was born and lived in the northeastern part of India in the sixth century B.C. The sixth century B.C. is regarded as one of the most significant periods in our entire human history since the great thinkers in the East were born in it; Gautama Buddha in India, and Confucius, the founder of Confucianism and Lao-Tzu, the legendary founder of Taoism, in China.

There are several names and titles for the Buddha. He is often called Gautama Buddha. Gautama was his family name; his given name was Siddhartha. He was also often called Sakyamuni, especially in the East Asian countries; it means the sage of the Sakya clan. He was also called Tathagata, "Thus Comes" or "Just Is," which signifies his absolute state of being. The most well-known title is

Buddha, which means the "Enlightened One" or the "Awakened One." Theoretically, anyone who is enlightened is Buddha, and all beings are potential buddhas according to Buddhism.

According to legend, Siddhartha was born as a prince in a northern kingdom of India. His father as the king provided all the best things for the prince. At sixteen he married a princess of a neighboring kingdom and had a son. Siddhartha was known as handsome in appearance and fair in color. He had wealth and power and enjoyed all the glory and luxury of palace life. Siddhartha's father kept his son from seeing any misery or evil in the world outside the palace. But young Siddhartha's curiosity concerning the outside world grew stronger.

One day he went out of the palace for riding and began to see some significant sights which changed the course of his life completely. The legend comprising these sights is called "The Four Sights." The first thing that Siddhartha saw was an old man with gray hair, broken teeth, wrinkled face and bent body, leaning on staff and looking very tired. The second sight was a sick person, prostrate and in deep agony. The third sight was a funeral scene in which people were mourning in great despair. Siddhartha learned that all men grow old; the beauty of the young will fade away like the flower and suffer death. The fourth sight was an ascetic, with dust all over his head and body, wandering in search for liberation. After experiencing these four sights, Siddhartha came to a deep realization of the horror and misery of old age, disease, and death as the universal and inevitable outcome of life in this world. This realization of agony and anxiety as the fact of life shook Siddhartha's mind so deeply that all the luxuries and pleasures of the palace life no longer appealed to him.

Hence, one night at the age of twenty-nine, he bade a silent farewell to his wife and son, and left the palace. Having entered the forest, he became an ascetic with a single purpose of finding liberation from the samsara world of old age, sickness, and death.

At the end of the six years of ascetic life, it is said, Gautama found no answer to the ultimate concern, and came to the realization that extreme asceticism is not a proper approach to spiritual search. He proclaimed the "Middle Way," which is neither extreme indulgence in luxury nor extreme mortification of body, as the proper way of attaining the spiritual goal.

After meditating in the "Middle Way" for forty-nine days deeply under the Bo tree, suddenly Gautama was "Awakened," and he became "Buddha," according to Buddhist legend. He then went to his home town and preached the so-called gospel of enlightenment for forty-five years until his death at the age of eighty.

Buddhism developed by Gautama was a challenge to the ritualistic and speculative tendencies of Hinduism. Against the discriminatory ideas of the Hindu caste system and the religious authority of Brahman caste, Buddhism also presented the democratic ideal of equality of all men in achieving Buddhahood and Nirvana.

In the teaching of Buddha the elements of divine grace for man's salvation were lacking, and Buddha often avoided metaphysical speculations. Buddhism was in the beginning a religion of self-effort, and basically a therapeutic and individualistic philosophy rather than a rational and metaphysical philosophy. Buddhism is essentially a pragmatism with a psychological turn. Since belief in God is not essential and God is neither absolute nor ultimate in Buddhism, some people call it atheism. In Buddhism the Absolute and Ultimate Reality is not God, but Buddha. This is a point of view markedly different from Hinduism, for in Hinduism, Brahman, who is God, is the Absolute and Ultimate Reality. This shows also a fundamental difference between Buddhism and Judeo-Christian philosophy.

The Four Noble Truths and the Noble Eightfold Path

The whole doctrine (Dharma) of Gautama Buddha is supremely capitulated in *the Four Noble Truths:* (1) That there is suffering (Dukkha), (2) that the cause of suffering is desire, (3) that the extinction of suffering is by the extinction of desire, and (4) the way to the extinction is the Noble Eightfold Path. These Four Noble Truths are the most fundamental, in fact the central doctrine of Buddhism. This doctrine is not a theoretical but a therapeutical truth according to Buddhism. To know the Four Noble Truths correctly means to know the essence of Buddhism. Gautama Buddha himself has demonstrated this in his preaching after the Enlightenment. To him, birth, old age, sickness, and death were the basic elements of the suffering of all living beings. He also included being attached to what one dislikes and being separated from what one likes, and being deprived of something that one desires. All these signified suffering to the Buddha. In brief, clinging to the five *Skandhas*, (heaps), which are the body, feelings, perceptions, impulses, and acts of consciousness, represents suffering according to Buddhism. And the cause of suffering is desire for pleasures, being and power, and this desire is nothing but the ignorance of man.[1]

Therefore, the extinction of suffering is possible only by complete annihilation of desire, radical liberation from lust and illusion of ego according to Buddhism. The path to this extinction of desire and self is called the *Noble Eightfold Path,* namely, Right View, Right Determination, Right Speech, Right Conduct, Right Livelihood, Right Effort, Right Mindfulness, and Right Concentration. This Noble Eightfold Path is called "the best of ways."[2]

The systematic and habitual meditation on the Four Noble Truths is the fundamental task of the Buddhist life, for it is the supreme path toward the attainment of the Buddhahood. Therefore, according to Buddhism the Four Noble Truths and the Noble Eightfold Path constitute the essence of Buddhist thought.

Hinayana and Mahayana

There are basically two types of Buddhism in the world now. One is the Mahayana (the Great Vehicle) Buddhism and the other is the Hinayana (the Small Vehicle) Buddhism. Hinayana is called also Theravada (the Elder's Way), claiming that it has the oldest tradition. Geographically Mahayana spread in the North and East Asia; Tibet, China, Korea, Japan. Hinayana is strong in the South and Southeast Asia; Ceylon, Thailand, Burma, Laos, and Cambodia. Vietnamese Buddhism seems to be a mixture of both Mahayana and Hinayana. Geographically, Mahayana is called the Northern Buddhism and Hinayana is called the Southern Buddhism.

The Mahayana is liberal and the Hinayana is conservative. The word "the Great Vehicle" indicates that the Mahayana ideal is riding together in the large vehicle toward salvation, while in Hinayana each individual rides his own "Small Vehicle" to save himself. Thus, Bodhisattva, which means "Enlightenment body" who remains in the world to help save others is ideal in Mahayana Buddhism. On the other hand, in Hinayana Buddhism, Arhat, which means saint, who seeks the Self-Enlightenment, is ideal. While compassion is ideal in Mahayana, wisdom is ideal in Hinayana. The Mahayana Buddhists criticize the Hinayana ideal as selfish, but Hinayanists claim that they preserve the true and oldest tradition of Buddha's teaching and that Mahayanists departed from the original teaching of Buddha. Mahayana includes some metaphysical and speculative ideas, while Hinayana stresses the monastic life and tradition. Within Mahayana, the Zen School and the Pure Land School are most important.

To a large extent Mahayana Buddhism shares many of the fundamental beliefs of Hinayana Buddhism, such as the Three Marks of Being (Impermanence, Suffering and Non-Ego), the Four Noble Truths, the Noble Eightfold Path, the Law of Cause and Effect, the Transmigration, man's responsibility for his acts, the importance of morality and Enlightenment as the goal.

Mahayanists generally hold that they preserve the true spirit of the Buddha and more fully developed and more mature level of Buddhism, while Hinayanists stress the early historical tradition. In Mahayana the attainment of Wisdom is for the sake of others, and Wisdom, Compassion and universal Enlightenment are inseparably interrelated.[3]

The spirit of Mahayana Buddhism seems to have originated in India as the genuine teaching of Gautama Buddha, but it was developed largely in China, Tibet, Korea, and Japan.

BEING AND THE WORLD

The Three Signs of Being

The Right Knowledge is essentially concerned with the nature of all living beings and particularly with that of man. It is summarized in the "triple formula" of *Dukkha* (Suffering), *Anicca* (Impermanence) and *Anatta* (Non-Self). The Right Knowledge of these basic facts of life is essential to Buddhism.

Dukkha (Suffering)

Suffering is the most fundamental phenomena of life in this *Samsara* world according to Buddhism. It is a most distinctive mark of our world, in which every living being is subject to misery; namely, birth, old age, sickness, and death. Dukkha is both a physical and a mental fact of human life. It is rooted in the very existence of all living beings in this world. "All existing things are involved in suffering."[4] Particularly, suffering springs from the sensual pleasure of man. *The Dhammapada* clearly elaborates the origin of suffering or grief as follows.

From pleasure comes grief, from pleasure comes fear; he who is free from pleasure neither sorrows nor fears.

From (earthly) affection comes grief, from (earthly) affection comes fear; he who is free from (earthly) affection neither sorrows nor fears.

From (sensuous) delight comes grief, from (sensuous) delight comes fear; he who is free from (sensuous) delight neither sorrows nor fears.

From lust comes grief, from lust comes fear; he who is free from lust neither sorrows nor fears.

From craving comes grief, from craving comes fear; he who is free from craving neither sorrows nor fears.[5]

Buddhism emphasizes the fact of the suffering and its cause, and always attempts to analyze them in every respect. For this reason, sometimes the Buddhist view of existence is called "pessimism." Although the Mahayana Buddhism (Great Vehicle Buddhism) of East Asia sometimes identifies suffering and happiness with focus on mind and with synthetic approach, the Hinayana Buddhism (Small Vehicle Buddhism) of Southeast Asia stresses that our *Samsara* (reincarnation) and *Karmic* (action) world is full of suffering. This is so, because of the basic analytical perspective of the Hinayana Buddhism. Therefore, we are to deny this world, awaiting a happy world in the future, according to the Hinayana.

Anicca (Impermanence)

Impermanence is also a universal, fundamental, and quite obvious phenomena among all existing things in the *Samsara* world, according to Buddhism. It is said, "All existing things are transient."[6] All things are involved in becoming, continuation, change, and death. Movement toward old age, sickness, death, decay, and passing away; these five are the fundamental facts of the phenomenal world. Every effect has a cause. Therefore, the cessation of an effect is possible only by the cessation of the cause. This is the essence of the analytical philosophy of Buddhism.[7]

Gautama's teaching of *Anicca* was intended to avoid the two extreme doctrines of realism and nihilism, the belief in being and non-being. Belief that everything *is* is one extreme view, and belief that everything *is not* is another extreme view. Avoiding these two extremes is the doctrine of the Mean, "The Middle Doctrine." The essence of the Middle Doctrine is that everything is a *becoming*, a process, because there is no static moment in the Samsara world. In place of an individual, one can speak of only a succession of instances of consciousness.[8] According to Buddhist philosophy the substance of our bodies and souls changes from moment to moment, and therefore there is no permanence in man. The organic change in all living beings is always determined by pre-existing conditioning according to the Karmic law.

Anatta (Non-Self)

Anatta is another important aspect of Buddhist philosophy. It means "Non-Self," that is, there is no eternal and permanent soul as substance in man. Buddhism emphasizes that self is not a changeless entity, but it is really empty. We find this truth about Anatta in the dialogue between the king Milinda and Nagasena, in which Nagasena denies the existence of Ego, for Nagasena is only a name, a convenient designation for the hair of his head, his brain, his sensation and his consciousness, etc.; not any of hair, brain, nail, etc., of his body can be called Nagasena.[9] In such an analytical approach Buddhism negates the existence of Self.

There are many illustrations about this doctrine. Some of them are as follows:

> Just as the word "chariot" is but a mode of expression for axle, wheels, chariot-body, pole, and other constituent members placed in a certain relation to each other, when we come to examine the members one by one, we discover that in the absolute sense there is no chariot; (in the same manner that) the word "house" is but a mode of expression for wood and other constituents of a house, surrounding space in a certain relation, but in the absolute sense there is no house. . . .[10]

In such an analytical method, Buddhism (especially Hinayana) views the soul of man as void, for it is a component of various sense elements in a certain relation. And the identity of an individual consists only of a continuity of moments of consciousness like a river which maintains its constant form of identity, although in each moment every drop of water in the river flows and never remains static.[11]

With analytical approach, Buddhism explains the complex elements of the conscious existence of man either in terms of *Nama-rupa* (Name and Form), which is man's mind and body, or in terms of the *Five Skandhas* (heaps or aggregates), which are body, feeling, perception, impulse and consciousness. In such a way Buddhism explains the human consciousness without reference to soul as an eternal substance.[12] Therefore, by analyzing man in terms of various related elements, Buddhism arrives at the conclusion that there is no *Atman* in man as an eternal or permanent entity. This analytical view of man's nature is especially strong in Hinayana Buddhism.

Samsara and Karma

Samsara may be translated as Reincarnation or Rebirth. The cycle of birth and death is a basic mark of unreal life derived from Hinduism. But Gautama's teaching is not about the transmigration of soul, but only the transmigration of character or personality, as it has been somewhat implied in the idea of *Anatta*. Therefore, there is a difference to some extent between the Buddhist concept of Samsara and that of Hinduism.[13] However, like Hinduism, Buddhism also teaches that Samsara world is the world of suffering and illusion, from which man must be emancipated to attain salvation. In this respect, it can be said that the Buddhist view of the world is pessimistic like the Hindu view.

The doctrine of Samsara is inseparably related to the doctrine of *Karma* (Kamma), which means the law of causality, work, or action. There are Karma of mouth, Karma of body, and Karma of mind. One's state in the Samsara world characterizes one's previous Karma, because Karma determines one's future. If one sows a seed of bad Karma, he reaps bad results and he is bound to the "Wheel" of Samsara, the rebirth of suffering.[14]

The ultimate source of Karma is ignorance (avidya) in Buddhism. The sequence of the causes of these is expressed in terms of Twelve Causal Chains:

> 1. In the beginning there is Ignorance (avidya); 2. from Ignorance comes Action (sanskara); 3. from Action comes Consciousness (vijnana); 4. from Consciousness, Name-and-Form (namarupa); 5. from Name-and-Form, the Six Organs (sadayatana); 6. from the Six Organs, Touch (sparca); 7. from Touch, Sensation (vedana); 8. from Sensation, Desire (trishna); 9. from Desire, Clinging (upadana); 10. from Clinging, Being (bhava); 11. from Being, Birth (jati); and 12. from Birth comes Pain (dukkha).[15]

As a best illustration the doctrine of Samsara is compared to the transmission of candle light. Lighting a light from another candle shows that the communicated light is one and the same in the sense of continuity, although the candle is not the same. So Buddhism teaches that a man's soul is not reborn as a concrete individual substance, but only as the name and form is the character reborn into the next existence. But it is not the same name and form that is born into the next existence, for, by reason of one's present *action (Karma)* is another name and form born into next existence.[16] Here the Buddhist idea of "character" that is reborn is very ambiguous and difficult to understand. This idea seems to rob the responsibilty of individuals, since it negates the rebirth of individual as real substantial self.

Yet Buddhism insists that *Karma,* one's action or deed, determines his destiny. In actual intention, the doctrine of Karma and Samsara points to good Karma by which one must be liberated from the bondage of rebirth. For, according to Buddhism, it is only by one's own earnest and right effort that the attainment of Buddhahood or Nirvana is possible. Concerning the relationship between Karma and Samsara the Dhammapada teaches:

> All that we are is the result of what we have thought. . . . If a man speaks or acts with an evil thought, pain follows him as the wheel follows the foot of the ox that draws the wagon. . . . The evil-doer suffers in this world and he suffers in the next; he suffers in both. He suffers when he thinks of the evil he has done; he suffers even more when he has gone in the evil path (to hell).[17]

NIRVANA, REALITY, AND ENLIGHTENMENT

In Buddhism the Absolute or Ultimate Reality is described in terms of Nirvana or Enlightenment (Buddhahood). The Absolute or Reality is also described in terms of Tathata (Suchness) or Sunyata (Emptiness). According to Buddhism anyone who has extinguished his desire or ego (Nirvana) is the enlightened one (Buddha), and anyone who is enlightened is one with the Absolute Reality or Truth (Tathata). These ideas seem to be highly subjectivistic, speculative, and vague mystical ideas, although many Buddhists insist that they are neither speculative nor subjective, but refer to the state of Reality or oneness with Reality instead.

Nirvana

Nirvana means "Extinction," that is, the extinction of ego and desire. According to Buddhism by the extinction of desire and ignorance, the extinction of sufferings of birth, old age, death, disease, sorrow, and despair is simultaneously achieved. With the extinction of suffering, there remains only absolute quietness and peace, which is Nirvana.

Nirvana as the world of perfect bliss and absolute peace is the opposite realm of Samsara, the world of suffering and anxiety. Buddhism believes that Nirvana is "the *Summum Bonum,* the supreme good, the incomprehensible peaceful state."[18] It is the incomparable security free from all marks of the Samsara world. Therefore, one enters Nirvana when he is completely liberated from Karma and Samsara. And in Buddhism Nirvana is the highest happiness to be attained.[19]

In Hinayana Buddhism *Arhat* is the ideal, venerable person, who is capable of entering Nirvana, in contrast to the Mahayana ideal of Bodhisattva. Arhat is the saint who has attained wisdom to be free from self and desire. "There is no suffering for him who has finished his journey and abandoned grief, who has freed himself on all sides and thrown off all fetters."[20] The Dhammapada further elaborates the glorious state of Arhat:

> He whose appetites are stilled, who is moderate in food, who has perceived void and unconditional freedom, his path is difficult to understand like that of birds in the air. The gods even envy him whose

senses like horses well broken in by the driver have been subdued, who is free from pride, and free from evil propensities.

Such a man who does his duty is tolerant like the earth, like a stone set in a threshold; he is like a lake without mud; no new births are in store for him.

His thought is quiet; quiet are his words and deeds, when he has obtained freedom by true knowledge, when he has thus become a quiet man.[21]

Buddhism further stresses Nirvana in terms of Nothingness or Emptiness (*Sunyata*) with an analytical approach, for in the ultimate state of Nirvana all fetters of ego, desire, and becoming are completely destroyed and extinguished, and only absolute calm and perfect peace remain. Therefore, to the one who is emancipated from ego, the thought of "I" (Atta) does not occur.

Although Nirvana is accessible here and now in our mind, yet a continuous and permanent realization of emancipation or *Parinirvana,* the "Final Extinction" is usually thought to be attained after physical death.[22] Buddhism teaches that when a person meditates on the Four Paths faithfully and thus the possibility of rebirth-causing corruptions have become exhausted, he arrives at a state of not being liable to be reborn into the next existence; by the cessation of the lust consciousness he passes into Nirvana with perfect freedom.

Tathata and Sunyata

Tathata (Suchness) is the ultimate spiritual essence. It signifies the Absolute or Reality in Mahayana Buddhism. It is beyond all predications such as existence or non-existence and one or many. It is also beyond human intellect and conception and logic. Therefore, it can be best described as "Suchness."[23]

Suchness means, in simple sense, to see things as they are in their self nature, to understand them as they are in themselves. According to Buddhism, it really means the absence of the division between the knowing and the known, the subject and the object. It is in the ultimate sense a positive affirmation of oneness of all.[24]

According to Buddhism, this Suchness is, therefore, the authentic state of Mind. The knowledge in this state is non-discriminatory and non-dualistic, in which one's Mind is purified and oneness with the Truth is realized.

In Mahayana Buddhism the Buddha is often referred to as the Tathagata, which means "one who thus comes or goes."[25] The essence of Tathagata is Suchness, which is Truth or Reality. This essence is equally possessed by all beings. It is beyond destruction and discrimination—beyond birth and death. In this Suchness the Tathagata and all beings are one and not two.[26] Ratnameghasutra states as follows:

> Truth means that which is not falsehood, that is, Tathata. The true essence of all things is absolute identity with Tathata. Tathata is beyond all relativity, evil, and passion. By its nature it is pure, tranquil, permanent, unchanging.[27]

However, Suchness cannot be really designated as a separate something or as an object of ordinary knowledge. It transcends the ordinary senses, ideas, and definitions. Hence, Mahayanists call it Sunyata (Emptiness or Void), for it is empty of all relative predicates. Sunyata is Tathata and Tathata is Sunyata.[28] However, Buddhists insist that this is not mere emptiness or nothingness. Rather Sunyata is a positive conception in the ultimate and absolute sense, for it is identified with Tathata.[29] In the authentic realization of Sunyata one transcends both mind and self, and in one sense mountain is not mountain and river is not river, but in another sense mountain is mountain and river is river, seeing things in their true nature without discrimination. So in the genuine Sunyata there is Tathata, the Reality. When the illusion of self is extinguished, the True Self is realized. In this moment one can utter, "Dwelling in one's true abode, unconcerned with that without. . . . The river flows tranquilly on and the flowers are red."[30]

Sunyata cannot be understood by ordinary intellectual process. According to Buddhism, it is understood only by Prajna, the transcendental Wisdom or religious intuition.[31] Once Prajna is awakened, one knows existentially what Sunyata is. Prajna is radically different from the ordinary way of reasoning or intellect. It is the true source of all knowledge, according to Buddhism. With it one knows all things truly. With Prajna one can truly realize the Emptiness of self. This moment is simultaneously the realization of Tathata and Enlightenment. Here the Buddhist concept of Prajna is similar to the Hindu concept of it.

According to Nagarjuna, Sunyata means the identity of yes and no. Emptiness is the middle ground between affirmation and negation, existence and non-existence. The enlightened mind transcends the discrimination of yes and no or existence and non-existence. The truth of Tathagata is thus Emptiness.[32] Also, as all is Mind, Mind-only, all things are empty of ultimate content.[33] Conze observes, "The Absolute is Emptiness and all things are also empty. In their Emptiness Nirvana and this world coincide; they are no longer different but the same."[34]

Non-duality is one of the distinctive marks of Mahayana Buddhism. The Ultimate Reality is one, and not two, according to Buddhist thought. Only in the doctrine of Sunyata does this oneness of all things become real and clear. It is not scientific or rational truth, but religious or mystical truth, according to Buddhism. Here we can state that the Buddhist philosophy of reality is monism.

In a Mahayana sutra we find a clear expression of Sunyata as follows:

> Form is emptiness and the very emptiness is form; emptiness does not differ from form, nor does form differ from emptiness; . . . where there is emptiness there is neither form, nor feeling, nor perception, nor impulse, nor consciousness. . . there is no ignorance, nor extinction of ignorance. . . there is no decay and death, no extinction of decay and death. . . .[35]

Sunyata as the ultimate mode of the Absolute Truth is, therefore, one of the most important teachings of Mahayana. It signifies non-duality concerning subject and object, Nirvana and Samsara.

The Buddhist thesis here appears to be anti-logical and irrational, for negation and affirmation, subject and object, emptiness and form, and Nirvana and Samsara are all viewed as identical. What is "the True Self" in reality? There seems to be no objective proof for its existence or reality. The Buddhist claim of Emptiness as Reality or Truth is really paradoxical and self-contradictory thesis. It cannot

escape the criticism that the Buddhist philosophy is a pure subjectivism, for it claims that the truth is realized in man's own mind,
and all is Mind, Mind-only.

Enlightenment and Salvation

The ultimate aim of Buddhism is also expressed in terms of freedom from the bondage of unreal life. In Buddhism the realization of
this goal is called Nirvana or Buddhahood. It is the state of extinction of false self or the illusion of self, and awakening into True Self
or Reality. The salvation in Buddhism is achieved through this
Awakening or Enlightenment. According to Buddhism, in the very
moment of Enlightenment the old way of illusive or dualistic thinking ends and new Transcendental Wisdom (Prajna) operates
serenely. One's mind is no longer controlled by illusion or relative
knowledge, when it is awakened. For the enlightened person, only
Prajna is the guide.[36]

In the enlightened state, one sees all things with a pure and clear
mind from the standpoint of the Absolute, and he sees Reality without obstacle. His mind is that of Tathagata. He is one with Reality,
and there is no more discrimination or dualism in his thought. This
is the state of Enlightenment in Mahayana Buddhism. This is particularly true in Zen Buddhism. In the state of the Perfect Enlightenment one is completely and finally free from the bondage of ignorance, Karma and Samsara. This is the salvation in the ultimate
sense, according to Buddhist thought.

Mahayana, as well as Hinayana, recommends the Threefold Discipline; namely, Morality, Meditation and Wisdom as the necessary
means toward Enlightenment. While Hinayana stresses the individual
emancipation of the Arhat as the ideal, Mahayana stresses the salvation
of all beings through the help of Bodhisattvas and Buddhas. Mahayana
considers that the Hinayana concept of salvation may be too ego-
centered and narrow minded. The Mahayanists emphasize Mahaka-
runa, the Great Love along with the Mahaprajna, the Great Wisdom
as the key for the salvation of all beings.[37]

Hence, the idea of the Bodhisattva is very strong in the Mahayana
concept of salvation. For the salvation of all beings, the Bodhisattva
postpones his entering into Nirvana until all beings are saved, and he

vows to help and serve all beings. Therefore, the Compassion is the supreme motive of individual emancipation in the Mahayana Buddhism. Wisdom in Mahayana is for the service of others that all may attain Nirvana together.[38]

Hence, Mahayana aims to secure the salvation of all, as the name, "Mahayana," (Great Vehicle) implies. Bodhisattva represents the heart of Mahayana concept of salvation. According to Buddhism, he is ready to enter Nirvana, and, indeed, he is just one step apart from it; but he willingly postpones his own Nirvana in order to preach the Dharma (Law or Truth), to give strength and encourage the suffering mankind to attain Nirvana together.

Bodhisattva is closely related to the teaching of the Pure Land School, which is also called Amida (Amitabha) Buddhism or Amidism. The Buddha-mind is defined, according to the Pure Land School, as "no other than the great loving heart."[39] This school teaches that salvation is possible by faith and good works. The multitudes who are weak and unable to help themselves find the Saviour, Amida, who can lead them to the Pure Land or the Western Paradise. The only necessary condition is faith and merit. When the Pure Land School reached from China to Japan, Honen and Shinran taught that faith alone is necessary and sufficient for salvation. Shinran taught further that even a bad man will be received in Buddha's Land through his rich grace. So the grace of Amida and man's faith enable salvation, according to the Pure Land School. The constant and sincere repetition of a formula, "Namu Amita Bul" (Korean), which means "Adoration to the Buddha Amida," constitutes the expression of one's faith, and this would enable the believer to obtain merit to be born in the Pure Land.[40]

Salvation by faith in the grace of a Buddha represented by the Pure Land School is one way of salvation in Mahayana Buddhism. It is the way of another's effort or strength. This type of Buddhism is criticized by other Buddhists as not authentic Buddhism. It appears that in the thought of Gautama Buddha such a concept of salvation represented by the Pure Land School was lacking.

There is another way of salvation in Mahayana. It is the way of self-effort or self-strength, represented by Zen Buddhism and Shingon.

It teaches salvation through enlightenment, which is brought about by moral deeds and meditation. It demands earnest effort on the part of the practicer.[41] One must work out one's own salvation with diligence. *Zen* is the Japanese pronunciation of the Chinese term, *Ch'an,* which means "meditation." Zen Buddhism emphasizes meditation as the only road toward wisdom and enlightenment. The Zen idea was strong in Gautama Buddha's thought.

Zen School teaches no reliance upon any other's merit. There is no objective Buddha to depend on or believe in, for one's own nature is Buddha. There is no Pure Land somewhere outside oneself or this world, according to Zen,[42] for one's own mind is Pure Land. Zen regards the way of the Pure Land School as distant, round way, but the way of Zen as the direct path to Nirvana.

Zen prohibits relying upon any doctrine or theory or scripture. It teaches one to rely upon only the direct intuition or the transcendental Wisdom (Prajna) within oneself. Zen has no outside teaching or tradition to rely upon. It cannot be established by letters. It must directly point man's Mind, and, seeing one's nature, awake (be) the Buddha. Thus, Zen Buddhism disregards the real importance of letter text or doctrinal book. It emphasizes the importance of one's Mind, which is to be awakened or enlightened through Prajna. When awakened, that Mind is Buddha's Mind. The Enlightenment through austere moral discipline and arduous practice of meditation is the ultimate aim of Zen Buddhism.[43]

Zen is an inner art of meditation to attain Enlightenment by direct intuition without relying upon theories. Bodhidharma, an Indian monk, is the historical founder of the Zen (Ch'an) School in China in the 6th Century A.D.

Zen's teachings include a technique for the sudden path to Satori, which is the Zen term for Enlightenment. In Zen, meditation is essential. Zen meditation aims at identifying oneself with the highest reality. It repudiates intellectual reasoning. To assist the meditator a *koan* is given, which is a problem. It is usually a meaningless word or a statement of nonsense from the ordinary point of view. Koan is meant to be beyond reason and logic.[44] It makes one doubt and think deep in order to reach the Enlightenment. It directs one's thought into one single issue. Gautama Buddha himself had a great doubt for six years about one single issue: "Who am I?" and meditated under the Bodhi tree for it.

The examples of koans are "nothingness," "the sound of one hand," "One Mind, one Buddha," "What were your original features before your father and mother gave you birth?" and "Whence comest thou?" The koan is to be taken into one's deep consciousness, and by identifying with it the meaning will be revealed. So koan is a means of attaining the goal of Enlightenment.[45]

Zen cannot be defined in an ultimate sense, according to Zen Buddhism. It is living in a true and serene way. It is awakened consciousness in action. If you have Zen, you have no fear, no doubt, no craving in your life, but you have tranquillity, joy, peace, and freedom,[46] according to Zen Buddhism. "Zen comes of itself."[47] One must discover the life-principle, the Mind, and control it like a "bull," and then, ultimately one must transcend both "bull" and self, in which all merge in No-thing, and then one reaches Nirvana. This Nirvana life is then lived in the ordinary life of the people of the world that all may be enlightened.[48] This is the essence of Zen.

Here also we find the subjectivistic and anti-logical philosophy of Buddhism. In fact, Zen Buddhism represents the most radical form of Buddhism as far as the anti-logical and irrational point of view is concerned. Zen, in fact, loves paradoxes, especially in its method of koan, which means problem or riddle, and which has no apparent logical or rational answer to it. Zen claims that it aims at the transcendence of ordinary logic or reason and ordinary form of knowledge. But how then could ordinary people know whether Zen Buddhists reach a transcendental state of mystical and intuitive experience of Satori or not? Here Zen falls under the criticism of rationalism.

TRIKAYA: THE THREE BODIES OF THE BUDDHA

An important idea of Mahayana Buddhism is the Trikaya, which means the Three Bodies of the Buddha. This is the Buddhist Trinity. While Hinayanists regarded the Buddha as an individual and historical person, namely, the Gautama, who attained the perfection of wisdom and the Buddhahood in this life, Mahayanists consider the Buddha in three ways, namely: Nirmanakaya (Transformation-Body), Sambhogakaya (Enjoyment-Body), and Dharmakaya (Law-Body).[49]

Nirmanakaya is the historical individual, Sakyamuni or Gautama, who walked on this earth, preached the truth after his own Enlightenment, and passed away at about eighty years of age. According to Buddhism, his life in the world was a manifestation of the Absolute. Although Nirmanakaya is a human body, its real body is Dharmakaya, and all Nirmanakayas are united in the Dharmakaya. Since Nirmanakaya is the vehicle for the activity of the Tathagata, which can appear everywhere and at any time, it is called "Transformation-Body."[50]

Nirmanakaya is for the benefit of ignorant beings, but the Sambhogakaya is a manifestation for the benefit of all Bodhisattvas. He is the preacher of the most of the Mahayana Sutras. It is "Enjoyment-Body" or "Reward-Body," because it enjoys its fruits of labour and is enjoyed by the Bodhisattvas. The Sambhogakaya is the personification of the Dharmakaya and the idealization of the Buddha, and therefore, it stands between the Dharmakaya and Nirmanakaya. To some people, Amida is Sambhogakaya.[51]

Dharmakaya is the Buddha as the Absolute in Buddhism. It is Buddha's "Law-Body." According to the Yogacarins, the Dharma-Body alone is the true Buddha. The other two bodies emanate from it and are supported by it. The Dharmakaya as the One Eternal Buddha has existed at all times, but it has manifested itself in many ways to save the world.[52]

Dharmakaya is the eternal, universal, and unchanging Truth. It is Tathagata in the real sense. In Dharmakaya there is the perfect Wisdom, Prajna. Dharmakaya is also the personal being of compassion, and preaches the Law, according to Shingon.[53]

The best word to describe the Dharmakaya is Reality, according to Beatrice Suzuki. It must be realized by every being for himself. Every man possesses it. It is the real nature of all beings. In this respect, it can be called Tathata, and the essence of Buddhahood.[54] Ultimately from the standpoint of non-duality, "the world of beings is just the Dharma-body; the Dharma-body is just the world of beings."[55] All beings have the germ of Buddhahood in them, and the Dharma-body is found in every being. The road to Buddhahood is open to all.[56] Here we find again the fundamental monism of Buddhist philosophy.

KNOWLEDGE AND MEDITATION

The Doctrine of Knowledge

There are two kinds of knowledge or truth according to the Madhyamika School of Nagarjuna: Conditional or Relative Truth and Transcendental or Absolute Truth. The goal is to attain the Absolute Truth or Knowledge.[57] Yogacara School divides the knowledge into three forms: Illusive, Relative, and Absolute or Perfect. Nagarjuna's Relative Truth includes the Illusive and Relative Knowledge of the Yogacara School.[58]

Relative truth is knowledge concerning the phenomenal world, which is not real in the absolute sense. It is often illusion. Ignorant and egoistic beliefs and most of the conventional religious doctrines belong to this category. A good example is the analogy of a rope and a snake. An unenlightened man walks in a night and is frightened at a sight of something long and thin, thinking it to be a snake. It is a rope, and therefore, his knowledge is illusion. It is a rope made of straw, which is in essence not an absolute entity.

In Buddhism the absolute truth or absolute knowledge is seeing things in their absolute nature, and it is seeing without object-subject dualism but in oneness of all things. The absolute truth is also *Sunyata* (Emptiness), according to Buddhism. It is emptiness of relative predicates and descriptions. The Absolute cannot be defined by relative terms or logics. It is understood only by *Prajna,* the spiritual intuition or transcendental wisdom. The understanding of Emptiness by Prajna is Enlightenment.[59]

Meditation and Wisdom

In Buddhism, to achieve Nirvana, which is the goal of Buddhism, the faithful following of the Noble Eightfold Path is absolutely essential. Within the large context of the Path, one of the most important methods is meditation *(Jhana* in Pali; *Dhyana* in Sanskrit; *Ch'an* in Chinese, and *Zen* in Japanese). But it cannot be expressed in words or letters, according to Buddhism. The heart of meditation is pointing directly to the mind, for when the mind is enlightened it is Buddha. Dhyana is thus concentration of mind. Therefore, it can be called *Samadhi,* the concentrated state of mind in which absolute calm prevails and trance occurs. When the mind is quiet and peaceful, it is like the flame of a candle in the absence of the wind.[60]

In Hinayana Buddhism there are forty subjects of meditation: ten Kasinas (use of objects for meditation such as water, fire, air and color, etc.); ten Impurities, ten Reflections, one Perception, one Analysis (analysis into the four elements), four Sublime Moods and four Jhana of Emptiness. The last two kinds represent a higher state, using the mind only without objects.[61] The purpose of Jhana is to achieve absolute purity of mind; namely, emptiness, the cessation of ego and desire. It takes great effort on the part of the seeker. Only the earnest man is able to attain the goal. "Earnestness is the path of immortality. These wise people, meditative, persevering, always possessed of strong powers, attain Nirvana, the highest happiness."[62] "Through meditation wisdom is won."[63]

"Wisdom" *(Prajna)* is the highest virtue in Hinayana Buddhism. It is in essence the methodical contemplation of Dharmas. According to Buddhism, it is a transcendent insight into Dharmas and has power to extinguish the illusion of man, the thought of "Self" or "I" itself. According to Buddhism, when a man extinguishes his illusion and ignorance of "Self" through Jhana and Prajna, that is the moment of Nirvana, the realization of the Absolute.

ETHICS

Buddhism teaches compassion and righteousness as the essence of ethics. There are two main divisions: the ethics of the Buddhist Order and social ethics. There are the so-called "Ten Commandments" (or precepts) for the Brethren of the Order:

To avoid (1) the destruction of life, (2) theft, (3) unchastity, (4) lying, (5) the use of intoxicating liquors, (6) eating between meals, (7) attending secular entertainments, (8) use of unguents and jewelry (9) the use of high or luxurious beds, and (10) the handling of money. [64]

The first five of these precepts are fundamental even for laymen. These negative commandments are closely related to the doctrine of Karma in reality. If one acts evil, he will reap evil. This is particularly true in the interhuman relationship in Buddhism.

The social ethics of Buddhism seems to be quite similar to most Oriental ethics such as Brahmanic and Confucian ethics, especially in regard to love, kindness, generosity, tolerance, respect, justice, and thoughtfulness between parents and children, between man and wife, between master and servant, between teacher and pupil, among friends, and between laymen and monks.

The ethics of Hinayana Buddhism, particularly in the above inter-human relationships, must be viewed in relation to the Karma. If one performs good and kind deeds for his parents, teacher, or friend, he will receive the same treatment. If he renders bad deeds among them, the return will be the same. "If a man speaks or acts with an evil thought, pain follows him."[65] The Dhammapada repeatedly emphasizes the importance of avoiding evil and doing good.[66] The ethics of the Hinayana Buddhism is also related to the concept of non-self and Nirvana ultimately.[67] If one is free from selfish desire, there will be perfect and harmonious relationship among people. This seems to be the deepest dimension of Buddhist ethics.

Buddhist ethics is, therefore, man-centered. It is not theistic; it is not based on divine revelation and it is not predicated in relation with God. This humanistic ethics of Buddhism stands in direct contrast to Judeo-Christian ethics, in which divine revelation is the foundation and in which divine-human relationship is essential. In Judeo-Christian ethics, the violation of the divine commandment is sin. In Buddhism such a notion of sin is absent. Ethics which is not related to divine judgment seems to be a very fallible and weak one.

EVALUATION

The reason for great differences among the different schools of Buddhism seems to be primarily the lack of authority especially in the form of divine revelation. Unlike the Judeo-Christian tradition, in which the divine revelation is the absolute norm and authority by which all human interpretations and speculations must be tested and judged, Buddhism does not have an absolute divine revelation as the positive regulating authority. Thus, in Buddhism human speculations and imaginations have produced all kinds of different viewpoints and interpretations which contradict each other in many respects. Some

Buddhist schools have anti-metaphysical and radically psychological traditions, while others have speculative and metaphysical systems of thought. Many sharply conflicting viewpoints within Buddhism seem to indicate that it is impossible to find any objective ground for truth in Buddhism. Hence, Buddhism may be called a kind of subjectivism.

The Buddhist view of being and the world in general seems to be pessimistic since it seems to have a generally dark and negative picture of the world in terms of suffering, impermanence, and non-self. The Buddhist concept of samsara is somewhat deterministic like that of Hinduism. History, time, and the world have neither positive purpose nor positive meaning in the Buddhist picture of samsara. This is another significant point which is sharply different from the Judeo-Christian philosophy of man and the world. God's creation is good, and man is the image of God, even after the Fall, although the original perfection was lost, and the world is real and has positive meaning and purpose, according to Judeo-Christian philosophy.

The Buddhist concept of salvation is generally a psychological change of the state of man's mind. It is expressed in terms of the extinction of ego or desire (Nirvana) and the awakening of mind (Buddhahood). It is also expressed in terms of the realization of Sunyata (Emptiness) as Truth and Tathata (Suchness) as the Absolute and Reality. Ultimately all these terms seem to point to man's authentic state of mind and nothing more. There seems to be no empirical or substantial evidence for proof that the Buddhist realization of Nirvana, Buddhahood, Sunyata, and Tathata is more than a mere speculative and subjectivistic theory. One interesting point to observe here is that the Buddhist claim of Tathata as Reality appears to have some similarity to the Platonic concept of Idea(s) as real.

The Buddhist notion of salvation is essentially humanistic. The so-called enlightenment is possible through man's own effort, although some Buddhist schools have the idea of divine grace and human faith for salvation. This is another point which is fundamentally different from the Judeo-Christian view of salvation in which the divine grace is the absolute necessity. In Christianity the concept of sin as disobedience to God is definitive and distinct. In Buddhism, however, such a concept of sin is totally absent. In contrast to the basically theistic picture of the world, man, and salvation in the Judeo-Christian philosophy, we find the basically humanistic picture of the world, man, and salvation in Buddhism.

FOOTNOTES

[1]Edward Conze, *Buddhism: Its Essence and Development* (New York: Harper Torchbooks, 1965), p. 43.

[2]*Ibid.; The Dhammapada,* trans. Irving Babbitt (New York: A New Directions Paperbook, 1936), v. 273.

[3]Cf. Beatrice L. Suzuki, *Mahayana Buddhism* (New York: Collier Books, 1963) p. 21.

[4]*Dhammapada,* v. 278.

[5]*Ibid.,* vs. 212-216.

[6]*Ibid.,* v. 277.

[7]Cf. A. K. Coomaraswamy, *Buddha and the Gospel of Buddhism* (New York: Harper Torchbooks, 1964), p. 94.

[8]*Ibid.,* pp. 94-95.

[9]H. C. Warren (trans.), *Buddhism in Translations* (New York: Atheneum, 1963), pp. 129ff.

[10]*Ibid.,* p. 133.

[11]Coomaraswamy, pp. 98-99.

[12]*Ibid.*

[13]*Ibid.,* p. 106.

[14]Warren, p. 232.

[15]Suzuki, *op. cit.*

[16]*Ibid.,* pp. 234f.

[17]*Dhammapada,* vs. 1, 17.

[18]Warren, p. 336.

[19]*Dhammapada,* vs. 203ff.

[20]*Ibid.,* v. 9.

[21]*Ibid.,* vs. 93-96.

[22]Coomaraswamy, pp. 122f.

[23]Christmas Humphreys, *Buddhism* (Baltimore: Penguin Books, 1962), p. 148.

[24]Suzuki, p. 42.

[25]*Ibid.*

[26]D. T. Suzuki, *Zen Buddhism,* ed. by W. Barrett (Garden City, N.Y.: Doubleday Anchor Books, 1956), p. 270.

[27]B. L. Suzuki, p. 121.

[28]*Ibid.,* p. 44; D. T. Suzuki, p. 263.

[29]D. T. Suzuki, p. 270.; B. L. Suzuki, pp. 44-45.

[30]Paul Reps (comp.), *Zen Flesh, Zen Bones* (Garden City, N.Y.: Doubleday Anchor Books, n.d.), p. 152.

[31]Humphreys, p. 149.

[32]Conze, p. 132.

[33]Humphreys, p. 17.

[34]Conze, *op. cit.*

35Edward Conze (ed.), *Buddhist Texts Through the Ages* (New York: Harper Torchbooks, 1964), p. 152.

36B. L. Suzuki, pp. 74f.

37*Ibid.*, p. 76.

38*Ibid.*, pp. 76f.

39*Ibid.*

40Humphreys, pp. 161ff.

41*Ibid.*, p. 164.

42*Zen* here is used often to mean Zen Buddhism.

43B. L. Suzuki, p. 76.

44*Ibid.*, p. 91.

45*Ibid.*

46Reps, p. 4.

47*Ibid.*, p. 175.

48*Ibid.*, pp. 133ff.

49B. L. Suzuki, pp. 52f.

50*Ibid.*, pp. 53ff

51*Ibid.*, p. 56.

52Conze, *Buddhism*, p. 172.

53*Buddhist Texts Through the Ages*, p. 182.

54B. L. Suzuki, p. 58.

55*Buddhist Texts Through the Ages*, p. 182.

56*Ibid.*, p. 181.

57B. L. Suzuki, pp. 39f.

58*Ibid.*

59*Ibid.*, pp. 40f.

60Conze, *Buddhism*, p. 100.

61Warren, p. 291.

62*Dhammapada*, vs. 21, 23.

63*Ibid.*, v. 282.

64Coomaraswamy, p. 130; Cf. Warren, p. 397.

65*Dhammapada*, v. 1.

66*Ibid.*, vs. 5, 17, 94, 95, 116, 117, 126.

67*Ibid.*, vs. 160, 161, 165.

PART TWO

CHINESE THOUGHT

As the ultimate question of philosophy and religion, "Being" or "God" was the supreme concept in the West, and "Dharma" (Truth or Law) in the Indian traditions. But in the Chinese tradition, "Heaven" and "Tao" (Way) occupied the place of the highest reality, and especially "Tao" was the most important concern.

Chinese temper strives for wholeness in general. It seeks union of ideal and real, heaven and earth. Its perspective is synthetic in contrast to the analytic tendency of the Western mind. Harmonious and peaceful life with the sense of wholeness is the ideal life in Chinese tradition. Such a way of life is called *tao* and it is the essence and goal of the Chinese mind, at least in the traditional sense.

The Chinese mind on the whole was pragmatic and had not as much speculation as Greek philosophy. Chinese thought is generally this-wordly and humanistic. Its traditional thought was also poetic rather than being scientific and analytic. The Chinese language itself is not logical but poetic, not precise but suggestive; each character has meaning as symbol. It is said that the traditional Chinese attitude was for tolerance instead of dogmatic discrimination and ideological opposition, since the sense of wholeness led the Chinese mind toward the sense of relativity of particulars within the universal totality, although it appears that the present Communist China has become a radically anti-traditional and intolerant society.

The ancient primitive China had polytheistic ideas of gods and worshipped them through shamans. Shamanism has been a strong element in the East Asian countries since the

ANCIENT TIMES. SINCE ABOUT THE TWENTIETH CENTURY B.C. THE CONCEPT OF ONE SUPREME BEING IN TERMS OF "HEAVEN" *(T'ien)* OR "SUPREME LORD" *(Shang Ti)* DEVELOPED.[1] IN SOME CHINESE MINDS, "HEAVEN" WAS THE SUPREME BEING AND THE PERSONAL GOD WHO HAS THE ABSOLUTE POWER AND RULES OVER THE UNIVERSE, WHILE IN OTHER CHINESE MINDS, IT IS AN IMPERSONAL COSMIC POWER OR NATURE.[2]

LATER, THE IDEA OF *Tao* (WAY) BECAME MORE IMPORTANT THAN HEAVEN IN CHINESE THOUGHT. ESPECIALLY IN THE PHILOSOPHICAL TAOISM THE IDEA OF PERSONAL AND SUPREME GOD WAS DENIED, AND INSTEAD, *Tao* HAS BEEN REGARDED AS THE ESSENCE AND THE ULTIMATE REALITY OF THE UNIVERSE.

IN CHINA THE GREAT PHILOSOPHIES WERE BORN IN THE SIXTH CENTURY B.C. AND THEREAFTER. THE TWO MOST IMPORTANT PHILOSOPHIES OF CHINA, NAMELY, CONFUCIANISM AND TAOISM WERE BORN DURING THE SIXTH AND FIFTH CENTURY B.C., WHICH IS, BY THE WAY, THE SAME PERIOD IN WHICH BUDDHISM AND JAINISM WERE BORN IN INDIA.

 CONFUCIANISM

INTRODUCTION

A MONG ALL THE philosophies and religions of China, Confucianism has been most important in terms of its cultural impact upon Chinese society throughout history, especially in the areas of ethics, politics, literature, and arts. It was the official philosophy of China for about two thousand years until the birth of the Republic of China in 1911. Confucianism was founded by Confucius, which is the latinization of Kung-Fu-Tzu, who lived from 551 B.C. to 479 B.C. Confucius lived about one century before Socrates. Like Socrates, Confucius emphasized the importance of virtue and knowledge. But probably Confucius was much less speculative and less rational than Socrates.

Like Gautama Buddha, Confucius was basically a humanist and pragmatist; both of them often avoided speculation about the meta-physical ideas of God or Supreme Being. Although it is possible to state that the Buddha had a sort of speculative metaphysical and eschatological ideas of Nirvana and Buddhahood, Confucius had little or no such speculation. Hence, we may state that Confucius' philosophy was more this-wordly and pragmatic than the Buddha's. But, in a sense, Confucius was a less radical humanist than the Buddha, since Confucius recognized the existence of "Heaven" as a sort of Supreme Being who rules over man and the world (although Confucius' idea of "Heaven" was not as sharply and well defined as the personal God in the Judeo-Christian theology), while the Buddha denied any such idea of God or Heaven as the Supreme Being or Ultimate Reality. Thus, it is possible to call Buddhism a form of atheism, but it is not possible to call Confucianism atheistic.

Buddhism was somewhat pessimistic about this world (although Zen Buddhism identifies this world with Nirvana existentially), since it stressed the nature of this world as the wheel of suffering, and the goal of life as the extinction of self (Nirvana). In contrast to this, Confucianism strongly affirmed the nature of the world as real and the goal of life as the realization of a virtuous, happy and peaceful life in this world.

Confucius grew up as a commoner at the time when the old feudalism of the Chou Dynasty was in deep trouble politically, socially, and morally. He had humble circumstances from his childhood. His father died when Confucius was a child, and Confucius grew up under the care of his mother. Hence, Confucius learned poverty and hardship of life from his early age, and this experience was probably one of the major reasons for his strong desire and search for an ideal life and world. His early hardships in life must have given him a deep democratic sense of sympathy for the suffering masses of the time. Confucius seems to have been a self-taught man.

The time in which Confucius lived is called the Period of the Warring States, which is also called the Spring and Autumn Period, 8th-3rd Century B.C. China was then not yet unified, but divided into many states which were warring among themselves for gaining more territories. As the consequence of the war, China experienced social, political, economic, and moral chaos. The major question of the time was: how can we live in peace? The question was the same among all men, but answers varied according to the different thinkers. The Legalists advocated the absolute power of ruler and the totalitarian control of the state by a radical form of law and order, while others like the Taoists claimed naturalistic individualism as the solution for the problem. Others like Mo Tzu advocated equal and universal love as the solution. Confucianism stood in the middle as neither extreme individualism, which sounded like anarchism, nor extreme legalistic and dictatorial totalitarianism, but as a mild and moderate form of law and order philosophy with a great concern and emphasis on the well being of individuals through compassion, kindness, and justice. According to Confucianism, the problem must be solved beginning with the individual, but the goal is a peaceful world. In Confucianism the family is the center, not the individual. Ultimately Confucianism triumphed over other rival philosophies as the official doctrine of the state because of its appeal to most people, especially to the educated rulers, not as an extreme but as a moderate philosophy for the general well being of society. Confucian thought consisted mostly of practical wisdom rather than metaphysical speculation. Confucianism was the greatest and the most significant unifying force of the Chinese people and of civilization in Chinese history.

Confucius' own life style was a living witness to his philosophy. He loved fellowship with people in food, drink and good song. He was cheerful yet firm, pleasant yet dignified. His life witnessed that his philosophy was a this-wordly humanism.

CONFUCIUS' THOUGHT

Heaven and After-Life

In Confucius' thought, Heaven and after-life were not denied, but were not emphasized. Confucius accepted what the ancient Chinese had believed about God and after-life. In the mind of the Chinese people, including Confucius, Heaven and after-life were not clearly and dogmatically defined, but vaguely recognized as real. Heaven in Confucius' thought was a purposeful Supreme Being, but it did not have a close and personal relationship with man as God in the Judeo-Christian tradition. Heaven was a distant Supreme Being who controlled the destiny of man and the world.

Concerning Heaven, Confucius said, "He who sins against Heaven has no place left where he may pray."[3] On other occasions, Confucius said, "I make no complaint against Heaven, nor blame men, for though my studies are lowly my mind soars aloft. And that which knows me, is it not Heaven?"[4] These statements show that Heaven for Confucius was a personal Being but very remote and not as intimately personal as the God of Jews and Christians.

Confucius also mentioned Heavenly Decree or Will *(T'ien Ming)*. He said, "At fifteen I set my mind upon learning. At thirty I stood firm. At forty I was free from doubts. At fifty I understood the Will of Heaven. . ."[5] In another occasion Confucius said, "The superior man holds three things in awe. He holds the Will of Heaven in awe; he holds the great man in awe; and he holds the precepts of the sages in awe."[6] The above statements show that the Will of Heaven was the will of the personal and purposeful Supreme Being. But Confucius did little speculation about Heaven.

Concerning spirits, Confucius had a more skeptical view. He worshipped ancestors' spirits as if they were present. He said, "To devote oneself earnestly to one's duty to humanity, and while respecting the spirits, to keep away from them, may be called wisdom."[7] When Chi Lu asked of his duty to the spirits, Confucius replied: "When still unable to do your duty to men, how can you do your duty to the spirits?"[8] When he asked about death, Confucius answered: "Not yet understanding life, how can you understand death?"[9] These references indicate that Confucius refused to speculate or give a dogmatic assertion of the existence of spirits or after-life, although he did not deny them. Here we find the basically humanistic temper of Confucius' thought.

Chun Tzu

In contrast to most religions in the world which stress belief in God as the essential task of religion, Confucianism stresses ideal human relationship as the essence of its philosophy. For this reason, some critics assert that Confucianism is not a religion, but a humanistic and ethical philosophy. Religious faith and metaphysical speculation about God and after-life were not essential aspects of Confucianism. Confucius was primarily concerned about the practical human problems.

The ultimate solution which Confucius conceived for the troubled society was that each member of the society, especially the rulers, must become *chun-tzu,* which means "royal man," "superior man," or "gentleman." If every member of society becomes "superior man," which is opposite to "petty man" or "small man," there would be no war and no trouble in the world. What then really constitutes *chun-tzu?* It is not a gentleman in mere manner, but in true character and conduct. There are several characteristics which make *chun-tzu.*

Jen

The most essential characteristics of *chun-tzu* is *jen,* which means humaneness, human-heartedness, love, kindness, benevolence or sympathy. Its literal meaning would be ideal human relationship.

According to Confucius, *jen* is love of man or ideal interhuman relationship.[10] *Jen* is one of the most important ideas in Confucian thought. It is often equivalent to virtue or morality. It is the manifestation of the genuine nature. It is closely related to propriety.

The *Lun Yu* (Analects of Confucius) states: "Artful speech and ingratiating demeanor rarely accompany *jen*."[11] It also states: "The firm of spirit, the resolute in character, the simple in manner, and the slow of speech are not far from *jen*."[12] It says again: "Once when Fan Ch'ih asked the meaning of *jen*, the Master replied: 'It is to love your fellow men.' "[13]

Yi

Another essential aspect of *chun-tzu* is *yi*, which means righteousness or justice. Confucius emphasized this in one occasion: "To see what is right and not to do it is cowardice."[14] On another occasion, he said: "The superior man understands righteousness *(yi)*; the inferior man understands profit."[15] Confucius said again on another occasion: "If a ruler sets himself right, he will be followed without his command. If he does not set himself right, even his commands will not be obeyed."[16] Hence, Confucius taught not only love and kindness, but also righteousness and justice in human relationships as an essential aspect of superior man.

Li

Another important aspect of superior man is *li*, which means propriety and ceremonies. Confucius emphasized the spirit of ceremonies rather than external forms. The important aspect of *li* is filial piety. We find the following teaching about *li* in *Lun Yu:*

> Meng I Tzu asked about filial piety. Confucius said: "Never disobey." Later, when Fan Ch'ih was driving him, Confucius told him, "Mengsun asked me about filial piety, and I answered him "Never disobey." Fan Ch'ih said, "What does that mean?" Confucius said, "When parents are alive, serve them according to the rules of propriety. When they die, bury them according to the rules of propriety and sacrifice to them according to the rules of propriety."[17]

Confucius stressed propriety in all aspects of life; seeing, hearing, speaking, and conduct. Superior man should know what and how to speak in accordance with place and time. He does not violate the moral standard. While *jen* is associated with freedom, *li* is a regulatory principle and law of human conduct. Reverence for parents and elders, ancestor worship, and reverence for Heaven are important parts of *li* in Confucianism. If a person does not know to observe *li,* he is not superior man. *Li* has the function of deepening the sense of reverence, awe, and transcendent meaning of life beyond the present existence.

The above ideas of Confucius indicate that Confucius' thought was man-centered and strongly this-worldly. His philosophy was thus a type of humanism. He did not deny the existence of God, spirits or after-life, but he tried to avoid or minimize speculation about them. He was partially an idealist and partially a pragmatist. His philosophy was an attempt to achieve harmony between the ideal and the real, between Heaven and man, always with more emphasis on reality and man. It seems that he overlooked the profound desire of man for life hereafter and God, since he put more emphasis on man's duty on earth than on man's spiritual destiny in relation with God.

MENCIUS

Mencius, which is the latinization of Meng Tzu (371–289 B.C.?), was the greatest successor of Confucius' thought. He systematized Confucian philosophy. Like Confucius, Mencius lived in a period of political, social, moral and ideological chaos. Like Confucius, Mencius traveled for many years to offer advice to rulers for moral leadership and government. Mencius' thought is based on Confucius' teachings.

Mencius' unique thought is his definitive emphasis on the original nature of man as good. He advocated that man possesses the innate knowledge of good and natural ability to do good. Evil, according to Mencius, is *a posteriori* product due to the external influence. Mencius said:

> Man's nature is naturally good just as water naturally flows downward. There is no man without this good nature; neither is there water that does not flow downward. Now you can strike water and cause it to splash upward over your forehead, and by damming and leading it, you can force it uphill. Is this the nature of water? It is the forced

circumstance that makes it to do so. Man can be made to do evil, for his nature can be treated in the same way.[18]

Here Mencius' analogy between water and human nature seems to have a fatal weakness, since there is no way to prove convincingly that such an analogy is logically or factually valid. A critic could argue in an opposite way that the forced circumstances makes man to do good, while his original nature is evil.

The following argument of Mencius seems to have some strong points and original insights, and is thus somewhat convincing:

> If you let people follow their feelings (original nature), they will be able to do good. This is what is meant by saying that human nature is good. If man does evil, it is not the fault of his natural endowment. The feeling of commiseration is found in all men; the feeling of shame and dislike is found in all men; the feeling of respect and reverence is found in all men; and the feeling of right and wrong is found in all men. The feeling of commiseration is what we call humanity; the feeling of shame and dislike is what we call righteousness; the feeling of respect and reverence is what we call propriety *(li)* and the feeling of right and wrong is what we call wisdom. Humanity, righteousness, propriety, and wisdom are not drilled into us from outside. We originally have them with us. Only we do not think (to find them). Therefore it is said, 'Seek and you will find it, neglect and you will lose it.'[19]

Mencius thus systematically re-interpreted Confucius' ideas of humaneness, righteousness, propriety, and wisdom within the framework of his theory of the original good nature of man. This served to enhance and support his theory. Concerning the nature of man Mencius speculated in great length as his major theory, while Confucius did little or no speculation on such an obviously invisible and indecisive issue. Confucius rather devoted most of his attention to tangible and practical issues, which Mencius also did later. Confucius did not advocate dogmatically that human nature is originally good, but he seems to have implied it to some extent when he taught the ideas of *jen, yi, li,* and sincerity of man. Since man is capable of self-cultivation of his virtue, according to Confucius, it seems to imply that man has at least the innate potentiality of good nature.

Mencius also advocated a primitive idea of democracy and revolution even in that rather ancient time. He emphasized the importance of the people and their will in the state, advocating that the purpose of the government is for the welfare of the people. He taught the idea of *wang tao,* "the king's way," which means the true way in which the king should walk as a high moral example and rule with wisdom, concern, sincerity, compassion, justice, and diligence. Following the spirit of Confucius' teaching, Mencius emphasized that the well being of the nation and a peaceful world are primarily the responsibility of rulers. The primary qualification of a king is the high degree of wisdom and moral character, according to Confucianism. If any ruler did not walk in *wang tao,* then it is the will of Heaven that the ruler is not qualified to rule and revolution can be justified.

Like Confucius, Mencius also mentioned the examples of the great ideal leadership of the legendary kings, Yao and Shun. At the time of their retirement, Yao and Shun had sought out a virtuous man among the people for their successor rather than leaving the throne to their sons. Heaven's will was the criterion for such decisions, according to Confucian tradition. Mencius interpreted the will of Heaven in democratic terms, saying "Heaven sees and hears as my people see and hear."[20]

Mencius had quite an original and proto-Communistic type of economic idea, too. He emphasized that a ruler is largely responsible for the economic welfare of the people. H. G. Creel shows us Mencius' economic idea as follows:

> A scheme very dear to Mencius' heart was one whereby a sizable square of land was to be divided, like a checkerboard, into nine equal plots. Each of the eight plots on the periphery was to be given to a family, while all the eight families were to cultivate the square in the center in common. The produce of the center square would go to the government and constitute their taxes. At the same time, these eight families would form a community with close relations of friendship and mutual aid.[21]

Mencius stressed that a worthy ruler puts in practice humane government and provides a secure livelihood, which gives a secure mind. In addition, a wise and virtuous ruler provides good schools and institutions of learning.[22]

Mencius opposed Mo Tzu's idea of equal and universal love as impractical, unreasonable, and unnatural. He emphasized the special duty of each individual for his family; the duty of parents for children, the duty of sons for their parents with special love, respect and service, the duty of a husband to love and be kind to his wife, the duty of a wife to respect and obey her husband, the duty of an elder brother to care for his younger brother, and the duty of a younger brother to respect and obey his elder brother. Confucian ethics was centered in the family first, and then included human relationship outside the family. There is a logical order in Confucian ethics. One must cultivate himself, and then rule his house. After he is able to rule his house, a person can govern the nation. After one can govern his nation with wisdom and virtue, he can expect peace in the world.

Basically, Mencius' philosophy is humanistic and ethical like Confucius' thought. His theories on human nature and economics are more advanced, systematic, and logical than those of Confucius. But Mencius' theory of the original goodness of human nature is a mere speculative hypothesis which has not been accepted by all Confucian thinkers, although his thought has become the main orthodox stream of Confucianism.

Mencius' theory of the original goodness of human nature implies that man can still have the original goodness and can restore it by his own effort and cultivation. This idea is contrary to the Christian idea of universally fallen nature or depravity of man and man's inability to restore his original good nature by his own strength. History seems to be a strong witness that man is incapable of purifying and perfecting his own nature, since there seems to be no substantial evidence concerning the radical self-improvement or steady progress of human nature or moral culture of human society. Confucian ethics on the whole seems to grant too much confidence to the ability of man to achieve the ideal society without any profound sense of depravity of human nature. Therefore, logically there is no need for seeking divine or super-human help to renew or improve human nature, conduct, and destiny.

HSUN TZU

Hsun Tzu lived in the third century B.C. Hsun Tzu's thought belongs to Confucian tradition, but it did not become the main stream of Confucian thought as Mencius' thought. The primary reason may be that Hsun Tzu took a view directly opposite to Mencius' concerning the original nature of man and an authoritarian political philosophy which in a sense gave birth to the totalitarian Legalism later. In opposition to Mencius' theory of the original goodness of human nature, Hsun Tzu advocated the original nature of man as evil. Fung Yu-lan contrasts Mencius' theory with Hsun Tzu's as follows:

> Mencius spoke of an ethical Heaven, and believed that man's nature *(hsing)* is a part of this Heaven. This is the metaphysical basis for his doctrine that man's nature is originally good. Hsun Tzu's Heaven, however, is a naturalistic one, and differs entirely from that of Mencius, inasmuch as it contains no ethical principle. In the same way his doctrine of human nature is diametrically opposed to that of Mencius.[23]

Thus, even on the basis of their concepts, Hsun Tzu differed from Mencius.

Hsun Tzu said: "The nature *(hsing)* of man is evil; his goodness is only acquired training *(wei)*."[24] Concerning the relationship between nature and the acquired, Hsun Tzu explained as follows:

> Nature *(hsing)* is the unwrought material of the original; what are acquired *(wei)* are the accomplishments and refinements brought about by culture *(wen)* and the rules of proper conduct *(li)*. Without nature, there would be nothing upon which to add the acquired. Without the acquired, nature could not become beautiful of itself.[25]

In Hsun Tzu's mind, morality is an *a posteriori* product of man through training. He says:

> Now man, by nature, at birth loves profit, and if he follows this tendency, strife and rapacity come about, whereas courtesy and yielding disappear. Man at birth is envious and hateful and if he follows these tendencies, injury and destruction result, whereas loyalty and faithfulness disappear. At birth he possesses the desires of the ear and eye, and likes sound and women, and because he follows these tendencies, impurity and disorder result, whereas the rules of proper conduct *(li)*, standards of justice *(yi)*, and finish and orderliness disappear. Therefore to give rein to man's original nature and to follow man's feelings, means inevitable strife and rapacity, together with violations of etiquette and

confusion in the proper way of doing things, and a reversion to a state of violence. Therefore the civilizing influence of teachers and laws, and the guidance of the rules of proper conduct *(li)* and standards of justice *(yi)* are absolutely necessary. Thereupon courtesy results, culture is developed, and good government is the consequence. By this line of reasoning it is evident that the nature of man is evil, and his goodness is acquired.[26]

Hsun Tzu believed that man can become good through education, although his original nature is evil. Man seeks profits from birth, and thereby men struggle and fight among them. Men become moral only after learning moral principles from laws of society and from teachers. Thus human nature is originally evil, and goodness is *a posteriori* product.[27] Hsun Tzu said further that the moral principles are products of sages and they are not products of human nature.[28]

Hsun Tzu's view of human nature begins with man's relation with economic issues. Man seeks satisfaction in gain and profit. Thus, he arrived at the conclusion that human nature is evil. This approach is different from the approach of Mencius who started from man's relation with man in terms of love and respect. Hsun Tzu emphasized human conduct too much in terms of "ought" and responsibility, but neglected the conscience of man and the natural love and kindness of man. As he overemphasized the responsibility of man, he became a rationalist, in whose mind knowledge was the highest value.

Hsun Tzu's philosophy is characterized as authoritarianism. He stressed that human society needs to be ruled by a strong ruler with a strong authority to achieve law and order. He advocated an authoritarian government.

Both Hsun Tzu and Mencius affirmed the ability of man to train himself to make perfect and ideal manhood, although they differed on the concept of the original nature of man. In this respect both Hsun Tzu and Mencius were really Confucians, for true Confucians put high confidence in man's ability to achieve perfection in nature and conduct, individually and collectively, without any transhuman help. Thus, Confucianism represented by Hsun Tzu as well as Mencius is a strong and positive type of humanism which is centered on man, believes in man's ability, and glorifies man himself. History seems to show us that mankind has been incapable of perfecting

his nature and conduct. Both Hsun Tzu and Mencius simply speculated on man's nature on the basis of their subjective reason. Thus, we
may evaluate their notions as subjective philosophy. Confucius was
perhaps a little wiser than Hsun Tzu and Mencius with respect to
human nature, since he did not speculate as to whether the original
nature of man is good or evil.

FOOTNOTES

[1]Cf. Fung Yu-lan, *A History of Chinese Philosophy* (Princeton: Princeton
University Press, 1952), Vol. I, pp. 30f.

[2]*Ibid.*, pp. 31, 57-58, 223-225, 284-286.

[3]*Lun Yu,* III, 13 in Fung Yu-lan, *Ibid.,* p. 57.

[4]*Ibid.*, XIV, 37.

[5]*Ibid.*, II, 4.

[6]*Ibid.*, XVI, 8.

[7]*Ibid.*, VI, 20.

[8]*Ibid.*, XI, 11.

[9]*Ibid.*

[10]Kim Kyŏng-t'ak, *Chungkuk Ch'ŏrhak Sasangsa* (History of Chinese Philosophical Thought) (Seoul: Tongkuk Munhwasa, 1955), p. 5.

[11]*Lun Yu,* I, 3.

[12]*Ibid.,* XIII, 27.

[13]*Ibid.,* XII, 22.

[14]*Lun Yu,* II, 24 in Wing-Tsit Chan (trans. and comp.) *A Source Book in
Chinese Philosophy* (Princeton: Princeton University Press, 1963), p. 24.

[15]*Ibid.,* IV, 16.

[16]*Ibid.,* XIII, 6.

[17]*Ibid.,* II, 5.

[18]*The Book of Mencius,* 6A:2 in Chan, p. 52.

[19]*Ibid.,* 6A:6 in *Ibid.,* p. 54.

[20]*Ibid.,* 5A:5 in H. G. Creel, *Chinese Thought* (New York: The New
American Library, Mentor, 1964), p. 73.

[21]Creel, p. 72.

[22]*The Book of Mencius,* 3A:3 in Chan, pp. 66-7.

[23]Fung Yu-lan, I, 286.

[24]*Ibid.*

[25]*Ibid.*

[26]*Ibid.,* pp. 286-87.

[27]Kim, pp. 71-72.

[28]*Ibid.,* p. 72.

 TAOISM

INTRODUCTION

Taoism as a philosophy occupies an important place in Chinese history. Its influence on Chinese culture was not as great as Confucianism, but it contained more profound speculative and metaphysical insights with respect to the nature of the Reality, universe, and man. The name Taoism is derived from *Tao,* the Way.

Lao Tzu was the legendary founder of Taoism. According to legend, he was a man of the Sixth Century B.C., about twenty years older than Confucius. *Tao Te Ching* (The Book of the Way and Its Virtue) or the *Lao Tzu,* which is the Bible of Taoism, was written by Lao Tzu according to some scholars, but others say that it was edited by someone else later. In addition to Lao Tzu's thought, Chuang Tzu's thought constitutes an important part of Taoism. Chuang Tzu is regarded as the real historical figure in the Fourth Century B.C. Chuang Tzu's place in Taoism is comparable to Mencius' place in Confucianism.

TAO

While Chuang Tzu did not explain in detail the concept of *Tao,* Lao Tzu explained it as a mysterious source, depth, or Ground of Being. The word *tao* is one of the most important terms in Chinese philosophy. It means "way" or "path." While in Confucianism it had primarily an ethical meaning, in Taoism it had primarily a metaphysical significance as the Absolute Truth, the Ultimate Reality, or the Eternal Ground of Being.

Tao Te Ching states as follows at the very beginning:

The Tao (Way) that can be told of is not the eternal Tao;

The name that can be named is not the eternal name.
The Nameless is the origin of Heaven and Earth;
The Named is the mother of all things.
Therefore let there always be non-being so that we
may see their subtlety.
And let there always be being so we may see their outcome.
The two are the same,
But after they are produced, they have different names.
They both may be called deep and profound *(hsuan)*.
Deeper and more profound,
The door of all subtleties![1]

Even at the early starting point of Taoism, a mystical idea prevails, because the Nameless and the Named, non-being and being are identified in Tao, the Ultimate.

The concept of Tao as the original source of all temporal phenomena is originally the unique idea in Taoism, which later made a significant and vast impact on the Chinese mind concerning the concept of the universe and man. *Tao Te Ching* describes the nature and function of Tao again as follows:

There is a thing, formless yet complete. Before Heaven and Earth it existed. Without sound, without substance, it stands alone without changing. It is all pervading and unfailing. One may think of it as the mother of all beneath Heaven. We do not know its name, but we term it *Tao*. Forced to give an appellation to it, I should say it was Great.[2]

Thus, Tao in Taoism is the mysterious essence of the universe, and it is also beyond the universe. It existed prior to the existence of the universe. While Confucianism affirmed Heaven as the Ultimate and Highest Reality both ontologically and ethically, Taoism regarded Tao as the Ultimate Reality above and beyond Heaven. Tao is all-embracing reality, and all accomplishments in the universe are due to Tao, according to Taoism. Yet Taoism claims that what Tao accomplishes is done spontaneously, not purposefully with any effort. *Tao Te Ching* states: "Man's standard is Earth. Earth's standard is Heaven. Heaven's standard is *Tao*. *Tao's* standard is spontaneous *(tzu jan)*."[3]

Fung Yu-lan, the foremost Chinese philosopher of the twentieth century, thus comments:

Thus understood, *Tao,* since it is the first principle of all things, cannot itself be a 'thing' in the way that Heaven and Earth and 'the ten thousand things' are things. Objects can be said to be Being *(yu),* but *Tao* is not an object, and so may only be spoken of as Non-being *(wu).* At the same time, however, *Tao* is what has brought the universe into being, and hence in one way it may also be said to be Being. For this reason *Tao* is spoken of as both Being and Non-being. Non-being refers to its essence; Being to its function.[4]

Therefore, according to Taoism *Tao* is both Being and Non-being, and it has a name and yet it does not have a name.

Logically speaking, this dual nature of Tao, that is, both Being and Non-being, seems to contain self-contradiction, although Taoism may regard these double aspects as the two sides of the same coin. Perhaps this is the reason why Taoism, like Hinduism, resorts to mystical intuition for the answer and understanding of the nature of Tao as the Absolute Truth and Ultimate Reality. There is a very interesting similarity between the metaphysics of Tao in Taoism and Brahman of Hinduism. Both Tao and Brahman are in essence and in themselves indescribable and nameless, while in manifestation and function, both are identifiable with many and all things in the universe.

Taoism never hides the mysterious nature of *Tao.* In fact, it glorifies it. The very nature of Tao is therefore called the Mystery *(hsuan).* "It is the Mystery of all Mysteries, the Doorway of all secret essence," according to *Tao Te Ching* as translated by Fung Yu-lan.[5]

Thus, in Taoism Tao is the original source of all beings and all phenomena. "Tao exists prior to Heaven and Earth; it is independent; it surrounds all things, it is mother of all things."[6] Tao is viewed as the absolute beginning and end of all things.[7] In formal appearance, this idea is strikingly similar to the idea of Logos in the Christian Bible, which is also viewed as the Absolute Ground of Being, and the beginning and end of the universe. But there is a difference in reality. For in Christianity, the Logos is personal Godhead, while Tao in Taoism is not a personal God, but rather the impersonal Ground of Being. The relation between Tao and the world seems to be viewed pantheistically and monistically, while the relation between God and man in Christianity is viewed in terms of the absolute and infinite Creator and the relative and finite creature.

Often in Taoism Tao is identical with Nature. This perspective is grounded in a monistic view of the reality and universe. All things are viewed as One, and the One is Tao. All things originated from Tao, which is One and return to Tao, which is One. This idea not only denotes the Taoist metaphysics and eschatology, but also it implies the Taoist ethics. According to Taoism, man's authentic life is to learn the principle and secret of Tao and follow its absolute law which produces the absolute harmony and peace.

Within the monistic framework of Tao, One Totality, there is a division of two opposite elements or principles, namely, *yin* and *yang,* which may be translated as feminine and masculine, darkness and light, negative and positive, or passive and active principles. Even being and non-being, high and low may fit into this category of *yin-yang*. This dualism is relative in Taoism, for it functions within the absolute contradictions, but is complementary in their final function for the productive movement of all things in the universe. This operation is called "Heavenly Way," according to Taoism.[8]

Power and weakness, being and non-being, and success and failure are all relative in mutual relationship according to Taoism. All things turn from life to death, and from death to life. This is a relativism and determinism. This philosophy implies that man's effort would be futile, for if man tries to weaken others, they become strong. Thus, Taoism teaches that man should choose gentleness and softness, which implies meekness and humility. According to Taoism softness overcomes toughness. This is opposite to common sense. The Taoist notion here in its formality sounds like the words of Jesus, "Blessed are the meek, for they shall inherit the earth."[9] However, the glorification of the meek in Christianity is always theistically oriented, that is, in relation to both God and man, and in obedience to the divine will, while in Taoism it is humanistically oriented and in reference to Nature as the model.

Taoism opposed Confucianism, because the latter stressed activism as virtue. Human effort to achieve happiness and peace through law, order, and education was emphasized and glorified in Confucianism, while it was regarded as unnatural and harmful in Taoism. In the political philosophy and ethics, Taoism was passive and negative, while Confucianism was active and positive.

terances in the Zen concept of nothingness *(wu* in Chinese
Korean and Japanese) and in the Zen use of paradoxes.
water, which is the most common symbol of *Tao* and *wu-*
are other symbols of *Tao* and *wu-wei* such as the Uncarved
), the Female, the Valley, and the Newborn Child. The
Block is a favorite symbol in Taoism perhaps next to water.
the natural state of being, simplicity, purity, and infinite
It is the model of man's original and authentic nature,
from hostility and aggressiveness. Here it seems to imply
affirms the original nature of man as good like Mencius'
he original goodness of human nature.

rved Block is described by Lao Tzu as blank, childlike,
s, and uncultured. This idea contains a mystical element.
of our growth and the state of Void and Quietness.[26]
bol of shapeless shapes, forms without form, and the
Way.[27]

oncepts of *Tao* and *wu-wei* are often expressed poeti-
and mystical language. In Taoism there is a tendency
rchism and radical individualism, emphasizing too
and passive attitude. In Taoism there is a radical
ltural perspective and anti-social and anti-system
stresses meditation and intuition toward the sagehood
. The authentic sage is immortal in Taoism, for
he eternal *Tao,* Nature. This idea of union with
Taoism as a Nature mysticism. While other ancient
ina emphasized law and order as a prelude to peace
ism emphasized individual freedom and *wu-wei* as
in the world. Taoist philosophy is exactly opposite
pe of philosophy in the West, which places high
civilization through the conquest of Nature.
not to conquer Nature but to be submissive to
The Taoist concepts of contemplation and intuition
significant influence on the Zen Buddhist emphasis
ntuitive wisdom.

Western idea of God, who is the personal Creator,
ge of the world, Taoism places *Tao,* which is
bsolute and Ultimate Reality.

Concerning the origin of the multiplicity in the world *Tao Te Ching* states:

> *Tao* produced Oneness. Oneness produced duality. Duality evolved
> into trinity, and trinity evolved into the ten thousand (i.e., infinite
> number of) things. The ten thousand things support the *yin* and em-
> brace the *yang.* It is on the blending of the breaths (of the *yin* and the
> *yang)* that their harmony depends.[10]

All things originated from *Tao,* and all things are produced by the
interplay of the two forces of *yin* and *yang,* according to Taoism.

Chuang Tzu states: "The perfect *yin* is majestically passive. The
perfect *yang* is powerfully active. Passivity emanates from Earth.
Activity proceeds from Heaven. The interaction of the two forms
a harmony from which things are produced."[11]

According to Fung Yu-lan, *Tao* is Non-being, as opposed to the
Being of material objects, is not a mere zero or nothingness. Tao as
Non-being is the essence or form according to Fung.[12] Furthermore,
Tao is not an individual thing, because it is the original all-embrac-
ing reality. It may be called Totality or Original Totality of the
universe.

The traditional Chinese concept of authentic power is *te,* which
means "virtue" or "power." Thus, virtue means real power in the
traditional Chinese philosophy. In Taoism *te* is always accompanied
by *Tao.* Fung states: *"Te* is what individual objects obtain from *Tao*
and thereby become what they are."[13] *Tao Te Ching* says: *"Tao*
gave them birth. *Te* reared them."[14]

WU-WEI

The power or virtue of *Tao* is expressed in Taoism in terms of
wu-wei, which literally means "non-action" or "don't do." It means
that Nature is spontaneous and effortless like a river. Applied to
human life, it means " don't take any action which is contrary to
Nature." Positively speaking, *wu-wei* denotes spontaneous and natural
action. It means that let Nature take its own course. Taoism emphasizes that Nature is the model or example from which man should
learn and which man should follow. The early Taoist philosophers
preached this *wu-wei* principle as the supreme political philosophy of

the sage-rulers. Holmes Welch interprets the meaning of *wu-wei* as avoiding the aggression.[15] *Wu-wei* denotes the humility and emptiness as the virtue of *Tao* and men who follow *Tao*.

The Taoist concept of *wu-wei* is based on the observation of the movement of the Nature:

> "The operations of Heaven and Earth proceed with the most admirable order," the *Chuang Tzu* tells us, "yet they never speak. The four seasons observe clear laws, but they do not discuss them. All of nature is regulated by exact principles, but it never explains them. The sage penetrates the mystery of the order of Heaven and Earth, and comprehends the principles of nature. Thus the perfect man does nothing, and the great sage originates nothing; that is to say, they merely contemplate the universe."[16]

The Taoist philosophy of life is thus opposed to any type of action or life that is a strain in any way. The Taoist simile in this case would be that the archer, who shoots badly because of tension and anxiety, when he strives to win a prize but is relaxed and effective when nothing of consequence is expected. The Taoist stresses that the highest skill operates on an almost unconscious level. This seems to be true to some extent, when the experts play piano or violin. But even the great experts need some effort to concentrate mind and strength to perform anything successfully. Taoism emphasizes the unconscious, intuitive, spontaneous, effortless flow of mind and action.

Concerning the true meaning of *wu-wei*, Welch gives the following interpretation:

> Every action produces a reaction, every challenge a response. This accounts for the rhythm discernible in life by which "the man who is to be laid low must first be exalted to power" *(Tao Te Ching* ch. 36) (pride goeth before the fall) and "whatever has a time of vigour also has a time of decay" (ch. 30).[17]

Thus, Taoism believes that wisdom is to ignore challenges and never to have aggressive attitudes toward Nature and men. According to Lao Tzu, man cannot achieve his aims by aggressive action. He said: "To yield is to be preserved whole. . . Because the wise man does not contend, no one can contend against him."[18]

Welch distinguishes Taoist quietism from
stating:

> A Christian returns good for evil in a spiri
> holy duty, and as an expression of his love
> Ostensibly, Lao Tzu would have us return go
> it, "requite hatred with virtue *(te)*" (63),
> effective technique of getting people to do

The most favorite simile in Taoism
the example of *wu-wei*. "Water is of all
overwhelm (rock) which is of all thing
Taoism thus praises quietness. *Tao*
eternal *Tao*.[21] Those who know do n
not know.[22]

> True words are not flowery,
> And flowery words are not true.
> The good man does not argue,
> And those who argue are not good.
> The wise are not learned,
> And the learned are not wise.[23]

In other places, *Tao Te Chin*
learning, we have no more tro
wisdom, and the people will b
The above statements show
of life, especially with respec
a sort of negativistic and pa
drawal. The above stateme
do not have universal vali
bad, but not necessarily ba
but some learned may als
which may not be bene
should be beneficial to c
does not have universal
practical life.
Such radical statem
have had a significar

similar u
and *mu i*

Besides
wei, there
Block *(p'u*
Uncarved
It denotes
potentiality
which is fre
that Taoism
doctrine of t
The Unca
dark, nameles
It is the root
It is the sym
essence of the
The Taoist
cally in vague
of escapist an
much freedom
form of anti-c
attitude. Taoism
and immortality
he is one with
Nature constitute
philosophies in C
in the world, Ta
the road to peace
to the common t
value on materia
In Taoism man is
and respect Nature.
seem to have had a
on meditation and
In contrast to the
Ruler, and the Ju
impersonal, as the A

In contrast to Confucianism which is *yang* (active) type of philosophy, Taoism is a *yin* (passive) type of philosophy. It seems that throughout the Chinese history, these two philosophies had a balancing effect upon Chinese culture, since many Chinese took their ideas as complementary to each other. But since Confucianism was less radically individualistic than Taoism, and since its ideas emphasized more human effort for the order, well being, and culture of the society, it had more markedly lasting and dominant and positive influence than Taoism on Chinese civilization.

FOOTNOTES

[1] *Tao Te Ching,* Ch. 1 in Wing-Tsit Chan (trans.), *A Source Book in Chinese Philosophy* (Princeton: Princeton University Press, 1963), p. 139.

[2] *Tao Te Ching,* Ch. 25 in Fung Yu-lan, *A History of Chinese Philosophy* (Princeton: Princeton University Press, 1952)), Vol. I, p. 177.

[3] *Ibid.* in *Ibid.,* p. 178.

[4] Fung, *Ibid.*

[5] *Tao Te Ching,* Ch. 1 in *Ibid.*

[6] Kim Kyōng-t'ak, *Chungkuk Ch'orhak Sasangsa* (History of Chinese Philosophical Thought) (Seoul: Tongkuk Munhwasa, 1955), p. 88.

[7] *Ibid.*

[8] *Ibid.,* p. 90.

[9] The Gospel According to Matthew, Ch. 5.

[10] *Tao Te Ching,* Ch. 42.

[11] *The Chuang Tzu,* Ch. 21 in Fung, I, 179.

[12] Fung, *Ibid.*

[13] *Ibid.,* 180.

[14] *Tao Te Ching,* Ch. 51 in *Ibid.*

[15] Holmes Welch, *Taoism: The Parting of the Way* (Boston: Beacon Press, 1965), pp. 33-34.

[16] H. G. Creel, *Chinese Thought* (New York: The New American Library, Mentor, 1964), p. 90.

[17] Welch, p. 20.

[18] *Tao Te Ching,* Ch. 22 in *Ibid.,* p. 21.

[19] Welch, *Ibid.*

[20] *Tao Te Ching,* Ch. 43, *Ibid.*

[21] *Tao Te Ching,* Ch. 1 in Creel, p. 91.

[22] *Ibid.,* Ch. 56 in *Ibid.*

[23] *Ibid.,* Ch. 81 in *Ibid.*

[24] *Ibid.,* Ch. 20 in *Ibid.*

[25] *Ibid.,* Ch. 19 in *Ibid.,* p. 92.

[26] *Ibid.,* p. 46.

[27] *Ibid.,* p. 47.

CHAPTER V

NEO-CONFUCIANISM

CONFUCIANISM, AS IT was developed by Confucius and elucidated by Mencius and Hsun Tzu, was primarily an ethical philosophy devoid of metaphysics. But since the introduction of the Buddhist philosophy from India, the Chinese mind began to speculate more about the metaphysical reality and life beyond this earthly existence. Taoism to some extent satisfied the curiosity of the Chinese mind regarding the metaphysical reality, but the Chinese mind on the whole lacked metaphysical and eschatological speculation. Thus, when the Chinese mind made a contact with the richly speculative and metaphysical ideas of India through the vehicle of Buddhism, it began to incorporate these ideas into its own framework of thought.

Confucianism especially lacked almost totally any metaphysical ideas. Thus, realizing this weakness, new generations of Confucian thinkers adopted certain metaphysical ideas of Buddhism and Taoism. Since the incorporation of metaphysical ideas into Confucianism is a rather new development in the Confucian system of thought, this new type of Confucianism is called Neo-Confucianism.

Neo-Confucianism is a strong development that came during the Sung Dynasty (10th-13th Centuries A.D.). It is essentially a combination of the Buddhist cosmology and Confucian ethics. It attempted to interpret the movement of the universe in terms of *yin* and *yang*, and the diagrams. The *Book of Changes* became important in Neo-Confucianism. The Neo-Confucian scholars thought that the Confucian ethics needed a firm metaphysical basis for its ethical ideas. Thus, they attempted to connect ethics with metaphysics. Another distinctive aspect of Neo-Confucianism is its emphasis on meditation, intuition, and the enlightenment of the mind.

There are several important thinkers in Neo-Confucianism, whose ideas dominated the Chinese mind for centuries. The most important figures were Chu Hsi, Lu Hsiang-shan, and Wang Yang-ming. Chu Hsi's system of philosophy is known as *Li hsueh* or the School of Principle, and the philosophical system of Lu and Wang is called *Hsin hsueh* or Mind School.[1]

CHU HSI

Among all Neo-Confucians, Chu Hsi was the most influential philosopher. He is generally known as Chu Tzu or Master Tzu. Wing-tsit Chan states:

> No one has exercised greater influence on Chinese thought than Chu Hsi (Chu Yuan-hui, 1130-1200), except Confucius, Mencius, Lao Tzu, and Chuang Tzu. He gave Confucianism new meaning and for centuries dominated not only Chinese thought but also the thought of Korea and Japan as well.[2]

Chu Hsi was a serious student from boyhood. He studied Taoism and Buddhism from his early age. His thought is profound, clear, and subtle. It manifests a vast scholarship. Chu Hsi's commentaries on the Confucian classics were regarded as the orthodox and the most authoritative interpretation of Confucianism for centuries.

The most fundamental idea in Chu Hsi's philosophy is *li,* which means "principle." This *li* is different from another *li* in Chinese which means "ritual," "ceremony," or "propriety." According to Chu Hsi all existent things are made up of *li* and *ch'i. Li* means principle or essence of things. It is incorporeal, eternal, unchanging, one, uniform, and good. *Ch'i* means material force, energy, matter, or substance, which is necessary to explain physical form, individuality, and the actuality of things. It is physical, plural, changeable, involving both good and evil, and is the agent of creation and change of things.[3] *Li,* according to Chu Hsi, are without birth and indestructible. They are part of the one great *li,* the Supreme Ultimate. Chu Hsi conceived of *li* as composing a kind of world of its own that is pure, vast, and formless.[4]

According to Chu Hsi, man's nature is his *li,* and it is part of the Supreme Ultimate. The *li* of all men are the same, but their *ch'i* are different. If one's *ch'i is* impure, one is foolish and immoral. This is Chu Hsi's concept of evil and its origin. One must strive for the purification of *ch'i* and gain the four fundamental virtues of humaneness, righteousness, courtesy, and wisdom. Chu Hsi said that by getting rid of one's desire he would be enlightened.[5]

Not only in man but also in everything there is *li*. A thing is a concrete instance of its *li*. Thus, without *li* there would be no thing. For Chu Hsi even dried and withered things possess *li* or the nature from the first moment of their existence. In the universe there is not a single thing that is without its nature. Walking on the steps, Chu Hsi said: "For the bricks of these steps there is the *li* of bricks." And sitting down, he said: "For the bamboo chair, there is the *li* of the bamboo chair. You may say that dried and withered things have no life or vitality, yet among them, too, there are none that do not have *li*."[6]

Chu Hsi gives another interesting example of *li* inherent in things without feeling. "A ship can go only on water, while a cart goes only on land."[7] Thus, according to Chu Hsi, *li* is inherent in all things before the concrete things themselves exist. Chu Hsi goes further by saying: "There are *li*, even if there are no things. In that case there are only such-and-such *li*, but not such-and-such things."[8] For example, even before the invention of ships and carts, the *li* of ships and carts already existed. Chu Hsi claimed that before the formation of the physical universe, only the *li* (principles) existed.[9] Thus, he gave an eternal, ultimate, and absolute character to *li*.

It is highly probable that Chu Hsi's concept of the *li* might have been influenced by the Taoist concept of *Tao*, for there is a striking similarity between them. In fact sometimes Chu Hsi equates *li* with the *Tao*. *Li* is empty and without form.[10]

Chu Hsi's ideas of the *li* as the essence of things and the *ch'i* as the manifested substance are somewhat similiar to Plato's concepts of "ideas" and "matter." For this reason Chu Hsi's philosophical system is called "the school of Platonic Ideas" by Fung Yu-lan.[11]

According to Chu Hsi, there is an ultimate standard for all things in the universe. It is called *T'ai Chi* or the Supreme Ultimate. Chu Hsi states: "Everything has an ultimate, which is the ultimate *li*. That which unites and embraces the *li* of heaven, earth, and all things is the Supreme Ultimate."[12] *T'ai Chi* is the totality of the *li* of all things. In Chu Hsi's thought the *T'ai Chi* is a mystical notion.

Fung Yu-lan points out that Chu Hsi's notion of the Supreme Ultimate is more mystical than Plato's Idea of the Good or Aristotle's God. The Supreme Ultimate in Chu Hsi's thought is not only the summation of the *li* of the universe, but is at the same time immanent in the individual things.[13] This is a dialectical and mystical notion, which is interestingly similar to the idea of a famous twentieth-century Protestant theologian, Karl Barth, who claimed that God is wholly transcendent and yet wholly immanent.

Chu Hsi makes a distinction between the nature and the mind of man. Human nature is the *li* of man that is inherent in the concrete existence of the individual. For Chu Hsi the mental faculty is the mind but not nature. The mind, like all other individual things, is the embodiment of *li* and *ch'i*. Mind is concrete and nature is abstract. Mind can have activities, such as thinking and feeling, but nature cannot.

Concerning his political philosophy, Chu Hsi claimed that there is the *li* of statehood or government. If the state is organized and governed in accordance with *li*, it will be strong and prosperous. If not, disorder and crisis will result. Somewhat like Plato, Chu Hsi emphasized that the ruler must be cultivated in the wisest way.

Regarding the method of spiritual cultivation, Chu Hsi stressed "the extension of knowledge through the investigation of things" and the "attentiveness of the mind." Chu Hsi believed that the method of "the investigation of things" would extend our knowledge of the eternal *li*. With "the attentiveness of the mind" one would attain the Sudden Enlightenment of truth and comprehension of all *li*.[14] Here Chu Hsi's notion is somewhat similar to the concept of the Sudden Enlightenment in Zen Buddhism. He was very probably influenced by Zen Buddhism in this respect.

Chu Hsi was a dualist since he made a fundamental distinction between the *li* and the *ch'i* and also between the nature and the mind. Other Neo-Confucian thinkers, like Lu Hsiang-shan and Wang Yang-ming, disagreed with Chu Hsi's dualistic notions. Chu Hsi was basically a humanist like all other Confucians. He attempted to provide a metaphysical basis for Confucian philosophy. He was a rationalist for he relied upon the human mind as the highest seat of truth and goodness. His philosophy is a sort of subjectivism since he placed the ultimate authority for realizing truth in the so-called Sudden Enlightenment of the human mind.

LU HSIANG-SHAN

Lu Hsiang-shan (1139–1193 A.D.) is the popular name of Lu Chiu-yuan. Lu Hsiang-shan and his follower Wang Yang-ming emphasized the supremacy of human mind in realizing truth. Hence, their philosophical system is known as the School of Mind. They both stressed that the truth is realized as a result of experiencing Sudden Enlightenment. Although Chu Hsi held this notion, too, Lu and Wang stressed this more than Chu Hsi.

Lu said on one occasion: "The universe is my mind; my mind is the universe."[15] In other words, Lu is saying here that without mind the universe cannot be realized as existing. This notion indicates that Lu's position is an idealism. Lu's position seems to deny the objective reality of things independent of the human mind. It is, therefore, opposite to realism.

According to Chu Hsi, "the nature is *li*." But according to Lu, "the mind is *li*."[16] Chu Hsi distinguishes the nature and the mind, but there is no such distinction in Lu's thought. Lu says: "Scholars of today devote most of their time to the explanation of words. For instance, such words as feeling, nature, mind, and ability all mean one and the same thing. It is only accidental that a single entity is denoted by different terms."[17]

For Chu Hsi the distinction between the nature and the mind is not abstract but a real one. For him reality consists of two dimensions, the one abstract *(li)* and the other concrete *(ch'i)*. But for Lu, reality consists of only one world, which is the mind. Lu Hsiang-shan's philosophy is a monism of mind *(li)*, while Chu Hsi's philosophy is a sort of dualism of *li* and *ch'i*.

Like Mencius, Lu was more interested in ethics than in metaphysics. Like Mencius, Lu maintained that man's moral cultivation takes place in purifying one's "lost mind" or one's true nature, which was originally good.[18] In this respect, we might say that Lu was a genuine Confucian.

Lu's notion of evil is also similar to Mencius'. According to Chu Hsi, evil was due to men's *ch'i,* an aspect of men's mind. But according to Lu, men's originally good nature became impure by external circumstances outside men.

Concerning the methods of regaining the "lost mind," Lu advocated that one must establish his own independent character, and become master of himself, and he must practice what he has learned. According to Lu meditation is essential for attaining knowledge. Meditation would lead to the Sudden Enlightenment of mind by which one realizes that one's mind is one with the totality of all things.[19] Lu's concepts of meditation and the Sudden Enlightenment here are similar to those of Zen Buddhism, although the goal of enlightenment in Lu's thought is different than that of Zen Buddhism. For Buddhism the goal of enlightenment is Nirvana, although one may say the enlightenment is Nirvana in Buddhism. But for Lu Hsiang-shan the goal of enlightenment is the attainment of the supreme knowledge of self and the world or the universal truth. In any case, it seems that Lu was somewhat influenced by Zen Buddhism.

WANG YANG-MING

Wang Yang-ming (1472–1528) is the better known name of Wang Shoujen. Wang Yang-ming is known as the most outstanding philosopher of the Ming Dynasty. Like most other Neo-Confucian scholars, Wang seems to have studied Taoism and Buddhism, but he maintained Confucianism as the true philosophy. Wang Yang-ming continued the philosophy of Lu Hsiang-shan, expanding it and giving a detailed exposition of Lu's sketchy indication of the mind-only-philosophy. He defended Lu against the charge of being a Zen Buddhist and endeavored to maintain Lu's philosophy as the authentic tradition of Confucianism.[20]

But when we consider his enlightenment experience, we can easily guess that Wang Yang-ming's thought was similar to that of Zen Buddhism as was Lu Hsiang-shan's. On one occasion while Wang Yang-ming was living in the mountains of southwest China, it was reported that he was suddenly enlightened one night. He claimed that through this enlightenment experience, he attained a new understanding of the central idea of the *Great Learning,* which became a basic literature of Neo-Confucianism among all the Confucian classics.

Wang reinterpreted Confucian philosophy and systematized the teaching of the Mind School.[21] It seems that the influence of the Zen Buddhist idea of sudden enlightenment is obvious in the experience of Wang Yang-ming.

Someone asked Wang Yang-ming, pointing at the flowers and trees on a cliff: "You say there is nothing under heaven that is external to the mind. What relation, then, do these high mountain flowers and trees, which blossom and drop of themselves, have to my mind?" Wang replied: "When you do not see these flowers, they and your mind both become quiescent. When you see them, their color is at once clear. From this fact you know that these flowers are not external to your mind."[22]

The following dialogue between Wang Yang-ming and his disciple also shows the mind-only-monism of Wang clearly:

> "The Master asked: 'According to you, what is the mind of Heaven and Earth?' The disciple answered: 'I have often heard that man is the mind of Heaven and Earth.' 'And what is it in man that is called his mind?' 'It is simply the spirituality or consciousness.' 'From this we know that in Heaven and Earth there is one spirituality or consciousness. But because of his bodily form, man has separated himself from the whole. My spirituality or consciousness is the ruler of Heaven and Earth, spirits and things. . . If Heaven, Earth, spirits, and things are separated from my spirituality or consciousness, they cease to be. And if my spirituality or consciousness is separated from them, it ceases to be also. Thus they are all actually one body, so how can they be separated?"[23]

From the above statements we find that Wang Yang-ming's concepts of man's mind and the universe are monistic. He emphasizes the oneness of man's mind and the universe. They are inseparable. This idea indicates that Wang's thought is basically a subjectivism, idealism, and rationalism like Lu Hsiang-shan's.

Wang Yang-ming attempted to connect ethics with metaphysics. He taught the three "cords," which are "to manifest the illustrious virtue, love people, and rest in the highest good." Regarding the illustrious virtue, he stated: "The great man is an all-pervading unity, which is one with Heaven, Earth, and all things. He considers the world as one family. . ."[24]

Wang Yang-ming taught that to love people is manifesting the illustrious virtue, which is to realize unity with the universe. With respect to resting in the highest good, he said: "The highest good is the highest standard for the manifesting of the illustrious virtue and loving people. Our original nature is purely good. What cannot be obscured in it is the manifestation of the highest good and of the nature of the illustrious virtue, and is also what I call intuitive knowledge."[25]

In Wang Yang-ming's thought the illustrious virtue is the original nature of one's mind. Wang believed that one should not study things but only their *li,* which is contained in one's own mind. He also emphasized the unity of knowledge and practice.

On the whole, the influence of the ideas of Buddhism and Taoism such as meditation, the enlightenment, the importance of the mind, and the *Tao,* upon the thought of Wang Yang-ming and other Neo-Confucian philosophers seems to be the major cause for the new development in the Confucian tradition. In some respects, however, Neo-Confucianism remained distinctly Confucian, emphasizing the humanistic ethics as the essence of Confucianism and sharply rejecting the Buddhist ideas of reincarnation, heavens and hells, Nirvana, asceticism, and pessimism. While we find the notion of immortality or after-life in Taoism, such an idea is completely lacking in Neo-Confucianism.

Neo-Confucianism in general and especially the ideas of Lu Hsiang-shan and Wang Yang-ming are highly subjectivistic and idealistic. Everything depends on man's subjective mind, according to the mind-only-doctrine of Lu and Wang. When man's mind is enlightened, suddenly he realizes the truth. A similar idea may be found in Buddhism, although in Buddhism the enlightenment of the mind has some ontological and existentially eschatological implications, while in Neo-Confucianism it has primarily an epistemological meaning, that is, a new intuitive knowledge of self and the world.

In the last several centuries in China, some new philosophical ideas developed, and Neo-Confucianism was challenged. The revolt against Neo-Confucianism came first from the thinkers of the School of Han Learning, such as Ku Yen-wu and Yen Yuan, in the Seventeenth Century. They criticized Neo-Confucianism as an abstract, empty, theoretical philosophy, and thus not the real Confucianism. They criticized the theories of the mind and human nature in the Neo-Confucianism of Lu and Wang as what they borrowed from Zen Buddhism. They advocated a return to the learning of the pure and authentic Confucianism developed in the Han Dynasty. They considered the commentaries on the Confucian Classics developed by the Han scholars as the nearest to genuine and thus the most authentic interpretation of the Confucian Classics. They claimed that the real Confucianism is the philosophy of action against the evils and for the development of a humane and a just society. They pointed to the examples of Confucius, Mencius, and other early Confucians as the practical philosophers. Thus, they proposed a sort of pragmatism as the authentic tradition of Confucianism as opposed to the metaphysical and rational philosophy of Neo-Confucianism.

Secondly, the stronger and nearer fatal challenge to Neo-Confucianism, and also to the whole Confucian tradition, came from Western thought. Through the impact of the West in the last few centuries, China changed more radically and more speedily than in any other periods throughout the thousands of years of her history. The Christian missionaries and traders brought to China an entirely new thought and new culture. The Chinese student who went abroad returned with a new learning. Sun Yat-sen, who became the revolutionary leader in overthrowing the thousand years old imperial system rooted in Confucianism and the founder of the Republic of China, was educated in the United States. He advocated the Three Principles of the People: Democracy, Nationalism, and Socialism. The tides of the West, namely, modern science, Capitalism, Democracy, and Communism, reached China almost simultaneously in the last two centuries.

Hu Shih, who was educated in American universities, returned to China to start the New-Tide-Movement for modernizing the Chinese culture. He was a pragmatist like John Dewey under whom he studied. He tried to reinterpret the traditional Chinese culture in terms of pragmatism.

Recently Communism under the leadership of Mao Tse-tung has been dominating China, radically transforming Chinese thought. To some extent Mao's Marxism is molded in the context of Chinese culture and society, but to a large degree it is Western in character. One may wonder how much of the traditional Chinese culture, and especially Confucian thought, remain alive in China today. Under the circumstances of the radically totalitarian system of Chinese Communism one can guess that only a small remnant of the Chinese past may be alive mostly in a hidden way. But since individual freedom is essential for the happiness of man, the yearning for this essence of man may grow so powerful that some day it may overcome the monstrous force of the inhumane totalitarianism that rules China now.

FOOTNOTES

[1] Fung Yu-lan, *A Short History of Chinese Philosophy* (New York: The Free Press, 1948), pp. 294 and 307.

[2] Wing-tsit Chan (trans.), *A Source Book in Chinese Philosophy* (Princeton: Princeton University Press, 1963), p. 588.

[3] *Ibid.*, p. 590.

[4] H. G. Creel, *Chinese Thought* (New York: The New American Library, Mentor, 1964), p. 169.

[5] *Ibid.*

[6] Fung, p. 296.

[7] *Ibid.*

[8] *Ibid.*, p. 297.

[9] *Ibid.*

[10] Creel, *op. cit.*

[11] Fung, pp. 294ff.

[12] *Ibid.*, p. 297.

[13] *Ibid.*, p. 298.

[14] *Ibid.*, pp. 305-306.

[15] *Ibid.*, p. 307.

[16] *Ibid.*

[17] *Ibid.*, p. 308.

[18] Creel, p. 172.

[19] *Ibid.*, p. 173.

[20] *Ibid.*

[21] Fung, pp. 308-309.

[22] *Ibid.*, p. 309.

[23] *Ibid.*

[24] *Ibid.*, p. 310.

[25] *Ibid.*, p. 311.

PART THREE

THE THOUGHTS OF KOREA AND JAPAN

CHAPTER VI

KOREAN THOUGHT

SHAMANISM AND THE TAN'GUN MYTHOLOGY

Shamanism and the Ideas of God

THE EARLIEST FORM of religious thought that developed in Korea was shamanism which controlled the Korean way of thinking before the introduction of Confucianism, Buddhism, and Taoism from China in the 4th century, A.D. Shamanism is not unique in Korea; it is common among Mongolian and other north Asian people.

Shamanism is essentially animistic. It considers that nature is full of spirits and worships them. It believes that spirits exercise super-human powers to bring about either blessings or curses. Shamans mediate between these spirits and men to bring about the blessings and to prevent or remove woes. Their functions were that of priest, medicine-man, and prophet in a primitive fashion.[1]

The idea of God in shamanism is basically polytheistic, animistic, and sometimes pantheistic. The ancient Koreans saw the vast nature with awe and fear as other primitive peoples did. This fear and awe eventually turned into worship and prayer. The religious conscious-ness of Koreans at this stage was primitive and superstitious. The deities in the primitive Korean religion were innumerable. The earliest deities Koreans feared and worshipped were the spirits of dead persons, deities in Heaven which were generally regarded as good, evil spirits in the lower world, and the spirits in nature. At this stage the concept of deities was ambiguous, and there was no clear theology. The ancient Koreans worshipped deities in Heaven to protect them-selves from evil spirits who were considered to cause all sorts of woes such as disease, starvation, and death. Shamans had the role of mediators between the deities and men.[2]

In the case of Korean primitive religion, there was one highest God among many deities. Koreans from the ancient past possessed this idea of God as the Supreme Being who rules the universe and governs the destiny of man. Koreans call this God in terms of "Hanunim," "Hanullim," or "Hananim." The first two terms imply God as the Heavenly Being and the last term implies the One Supreme Being.[3] However, essentially they all mean the same Ultimate Reality in the Korean mind. They are more distinctly personal in the Korean mind than the Chinese idea, *T'ien,* which means Heaven.

The ancient Koreans, therefore, had a primitive type of vague monotheism or polytheistic monotheism. It is different from the type of monotheism that the Judeo-Christian tradition maintains. The Judeo-Christian monotheism may be called a pure and absolute monotheism, for in the Judeo-Christian tradition, *Yahweh* alone is the only true God, while in the Korean tradition, *Hananim* is not necessarily the only true God over against other gods. Koreans worshipped *Hananim* for the blessings of rain and harvest which were most important for the agriculturally-oriented people in traditional Korea. Even today this is true to a great extent.

Not only did the primitive Koreans regard *Hananim* as the highest deity, but also Confucianists and Buddhists in Korea regarded him as such; and Christians in Korea adopted the same word to designate their God. Most Koreans regard *Hananim* as the Supreme Being today. However, in Korean shamanism the concept of the Supreme Being is not well developed. The primitive Koreans assumed without a clear idea or doctrine that *Hananim* created and rules the universe. But he is remote from the world and does not interfere with every detail of the daily life of man. Thus, the primitive Koreans worshipped other deities who were regarded as the controllers of many things. Mountain gods, river gods, and the spirits of ancestors were typical ones. There were good and evil spirits, and all the gods and spirits were regarded as having super-human powers. They were invisible to common people, but were considered as visible to shamans, who could be either male or female. Shamans *(mutang)* played the role of mediator for the common people.[4]

The concept of the universe in Korean shamanism is interesting.

The universe consists of three stories: the high world, the middle world, and the low world. The high world is the world of heaven and light, where the highest deity and good spirits reside. The middle world is the world of man and animals. The low world is hell where the evil spirits reside. Korean shamanism believed that one ascends into the high world or descends to the low world according to one's deeds in the present life.[5] Thus, even in Korean shamanism one may find a primitive and simple concept of after-life and ethics; but there is no refined doctrine of sin, judgment, and ethics in the primitive religion of Korea. These primitive ideas were easily incorporated into Buddhism and Confucianism in Korea later, since they were simple notions.

The Tan'gun Mythology

Tan'gun mythology is a theory of the origin of Korea as a nation. It is recorded in *Samguk Yusa* (The Events of the Three Kingdoms) authored by Ilyon, who was a renounced Buddhist monk in the Koryō Dynasty in the 13th Century A.D. The oral tradition of the Tan'gun mythology might have existed from the ancient past of Chosōn,[6] the old Korea, probably about the Twentieth Century B.C.

The Tan'gun story is regarded as mythology by many scholars, but it is also regarded as a real and factual history by many Koreans.[7] According to the Tan'gun mythology, there was a Heavenly king called Hanin, who sent his son, Hanung to rule the world. He descended upon T'aebaek Mountain in the northernmost part of Korea and founded the Heavenly City. With the assistance of the ministers of wind, rain, and cloud, he ruled over human affairs such as grain, life, disease, judgment, good, and evil, etc. He married a woman who changed from a bear, and bore a son called Tan'gun, who became the founder of Chosōn.[8]

Tan'gun was both the religious and political head of the nation, in which there was no separation of religion and state. He was both king and priest (shaman). Tan'gun was divine-man in essence. Thus in this mythology there is an implication of pride and glory of Korea as a unique nation, since its founder was the son of God. Hence, in the Tan'gun mythology we find the primitive form of Korean thought concerning the origin of its nation and people. This mythology is perhaps the oldest and common faith of most Korean people. This mythology is similar, in some respects, to the Shinto mythology of the origin of Japan and the divinity of the emperor in Japan.

BUDDHISM IN KOREA

Introduction

Buddhism is the first foreign religion which entered Korea. Its first arrival in Korea from China is dated 372 A.D. The first Buddhist missionary to Korea was monk Sundo, who brought with him Buddhist scriptures and a Buddha statue. Korean Buddhism, like the Buddhism of most other nations, adopted the central teachings of Buddhism such as the Four Noble Truths and the Eight Noble Paths. But the type of Buddhism developed in Korea is Mahayana Buddhism like that of China.[9]

Mahayana is not as monastery-centered as Hinayana Buddhism. Mahayana aimed at the mass religion. It emphasizes the monism of universal Buddhahood. It does not sharply distinguish between Nirvana and this world. Rather it aims at the identification of the two. Its goal is universal salvation through Bodhisattvas, who help others to attain Nirvana. Mahayana stresses the emptiness as Truth and Beauty. The elements of Zen (Ch'an) Buddhism were strong in Korean Buddhism.

Buddhism was quite strong in Korea during the Silla dynasty around the Sixth to Eighth Centuries A.D. It was the state religion during the Koryo dynasty from the Tenth to Fourteenth Centuries A.D. Since the Yi dynasty, which began in the Fourteenth Century A.D., Buddhism declined under the Yi rulers who adopted Confucianism as the national religion and persecuted the Buddhists.

According to some Korean Buddhists, Indian Buddhism is an introductory stage like a seeding period, Chinese Buddhism is a developing stage like a blossoming period, and Korean Buddhism is a concluding stage like the fruition period. During the Silla and Koryo dynasties there were many brilliant cultural achievements of Buddhism such as the famous Bulguksa Temple and Sokgulam Buddha image. There were also many outstanding Buddhist scholars and monks who developed a somewhat uniquely Korean-type of Buddhist thought. The most typical and outstanding figure is Wŏnhyo, in whose thought one may find the essence of Korean Buddhism.

Besides Wŏnhyo, there were several other great thinkers during the golden age of Korean Buddhism. Hyongkwang, Wonkwang, Uisang, and other Buddhist monks went to China for study, and their learning and ideas all contributed to the great development of Korean Buddhism.[10] Among all Korean Buddhist thinkers, Wŏnhyo is best known.

Wonhyo's Thought

Wŏnhyo's thought represents the highest level of the original and characteristic aspect of Korean Buddhism and especially of the Buddhism of the Silla Dynasty.[11] The major characteristic of Silla Buddhism is its emphasis on the identity of the sacred and the secular or Truth and the world. Here Silla Buddhism is essentially Mahayana, in which Nirvana and this world are identified. In Mahayana it is not necessary to leave one's home and enter monastic life for salvation. Mahayana stresses the universal salvation of all men through enlightenment. The ultimate goal of Mahayana is the attainment of Buddhahood for all living beings.

Wŏnhyo lived in the Seventh Century A.D. His learning is regarded as broad and included even Confucian ideas. There is a famous legend about him. He was once traveling to China for study. On the way one night he slept near graves. He was very thirsty in the middle of the night and searched for water. He touched water, drank it, and was satisfied. The next morning he discovered that the water was in a human skull. Wŏnhyo suddenly realized a truth, that when a mind is alive, all kinds of truth can be born, and when a mind is dead or dark, it is not different from a skull. He realized that all things depend on mind. The night before, his mind did not realize that what he drank was dirty water in a skull. When the light came, his mind realized what kind of water he drank. Wŏnhyo realized that there is no need to go abroad in a distant place to study. Hence, he returned home and concentrated on the cultivation of his mind.

Wŏnhyo stressed the mind-only doctrine. He was thus an idealist and rationalist, for all things originate from mind and all truths return to one mind. His philosophy was basically monism. All things in the universe are viewed as equal, same and one. According to the dialectical monism of Wŏnhyo, phenomenon is essence and reality;

discrimination is equality; being is non-being; existence is emptiness; the sacred is secular; all beings are Buddha; and life and death are identical. Wŏnhyo's aim was to be universalistic and absolutely non-discriminatory. By doing so, Wŏnhyo's thought became pantheistic, and non-sense to common sense. To common sense Wŏnhyo's thought is paradoxical, absurd, and illogical, since he identifies being and non-being, and life and death.

With such a monistic perspective Wŏnhyo strived for a synthesis of all different Buddhist doctrines. Thus his philosophy was a syncretism, and his Buddhism was a universalistic Buddhism. He aimed at the transcendence of both being and non-being. He tried to avoid not only the two extremes but also the middle way. Where there is no middle, there is true unity and peace according to Wŏnhyo's philosophy. There is no difference between Nirvana and this world in Wŏnhyo's mind. All beings possess the Buddha nature. Wŏnhyo recognized that this philosophy is not a logic that can be understood by an objectivistic epistemology. Wŏnhyo considered that his philosophy is an existential logic.[12] But really such a Buddhist thought as Wŏnhyo's is a typical Buddhist mysticism, in which the ordinary logic is either dismissed or transcended.

Thus, we find that Wŏnhyo's thought is basically a form of monistic universalism. All beings have the Buddha nature and all things are ultimately one. One is many and many are one. Wŏnhyo's thought is also a religious secularism. According to Wŏnhyo the authentic religion is a secularized one. True religion is not escapism, but positive life in the world with freedom, joy, and service. Wŏnhyo's philosophy seems to be highly subjectivistic, at least according to the common rational standard. Wŏnhyo's philosophy may be called also an irrational rationalism, for it emphasizes the decisive role of mind for realizing truth, and yet it seems to love and glorify paradoxes and absurdity by either ignoring or despising the ordinary rational logic which clearly distinguishes between being and non-being, life and death, or the sacred and secular.

CONFUCIANISM IN KOREA

Introduction

Confucianism, as with Buddhism, was introduced from China to Korea probably in the fourth century A.D. Confucianism in Korea is basically the same as Confucianism in China. Korean Confucianism is based upon the classical writings of Confucianism, and its basic teachings are *Jen, Yi, Li* and *Chun-tzu* like Chinese Confucianism. Confucianism is basically a humanistic philosophy with the ultimate goal of achieving a peaceful world through the cultivation of individual character.

Under the shadow of Buddhism which had been the national religion of the Silla and Koryo dynasties approximately between the Fifth and Fourteenth Centuries, Confucianism did not have a chance to grow. But toward the end of the Koryo dynasty in the Thirteenth and Fourteenth Centuries, Confucianism was rising toward importance in Korea. Chŏng Mong-ju, Chŏng To-chŏn, and others helped to lay down the foundation for the Confucianism of the Yi dynasty during which Confucianism was adopted as the state religion.

Buddhism in the Koryo dynasty had the losing lot together with the fall of the dynasty itself. Buddhism lost leadership among the people due to its corruption associated with the political system. At the same time Confucianism was destined to become the ruling philosophy of the Yi dynasty, since the founding members of the Yi dynasty were very sympathetic to Confucianism, while they were strongly opposed to Buddhism.

The main stream of the Yi dynasty Confucianism was *Sŏnglihak* (The School of the Principle of Human Nature), which stressed the importance of individual knowledge and the cultivation of character, Sŏnglihak is basically a rationalistic and theoretical philosophy. In the midst of political troubles scholars often sought an escape and refuge in the study of Confucianism in secluded quiet places. Sŏ Hwadam, Yi T'woegye, Yi Yulgok are the examples of the great scholars of Confucianism during the Yi dynasty. Among them Yulgok was the most brilliant and famous. He developed some very significant original ideas.

Yulgok's Thought

Yi Yulgok (1536–1584 A.D.) is known as the greatest Confucian thinker in Korean history. Korean Confucianism is proud of his achievements. According to the testimony of history, Yulgok was an honest, calm, dignified, and indiscriminatory gentleman. He was famous for his devotion to the well being of the nation rather than his own personal gain, when he was in high positions in the government of the Yi Dynasty. Yulgok had a deep conviction that Confucianism was the best moral and political philosophy for the nation's well being. Yulgok's thought belongs to the large framework of the School of the Principle of Human Nature (Sŏnglihak). Before Yulgok there were other Confucian scholars in Korea who paved the way for this school. They were Chŏng Mong-ju, Cho Kwangjo, Yi T'woegye, and Sŏ Hwadam.

Yulgok's thought is not analytical, but synthetic in its basic approach. Yulgok's basic philosophy is synthetic monism. As far as this synthetic and monistic perspective is concerned, there is an interesting similarity between Yulgok's mind and Wŏnhyo's approach in Silla Buddhism. Yulgok's philosophy is a synthesis of Sŏ Hwadam's energy only monism and Yi T'woegye's principle and energy dualism. Sŏ Hwadam and Yi T'woegye were Yulgok's predecessors.

Korean *Sŏnglihak* is both metaphysical and ethical theory. It is a synthesis of cosmology and psychology. This, in essence, is based on Chinese Neo-Confucianism, and especially Chu Hsi's philosophy. Yulgok thought that the universe consisted of *li* (principle) and *ki* (energy).[13] This idea was originally developed by Chu Hsi (the 12th Century A.D.) of Chinese Neo-Confucianism. Yulgok's idea here sounds like a dualistic notion, in a sense. But according to Yulgok, *li* and *ki* are not really two. While they are one, yet they are two, and while they are two, yet they are one. Between *li* and *ki* there is an inseparable relation. The only distinction is that *li* is the essence or reality of the universe, and *ki* is the concretized functional aspect of the universe.

The movement or appearance is *ki,* and its cause or reason is *li,* according to Yulgok. Thus, Yulgok's thought is expressed in terms of the oneness of *ki,* the movement and *li,* the basis. In other words, Yulgok's theory is that the operation of *ki* and the ground of *li* have the ultimate unity, and they are not two realities. All phenomena have one ultimate origin in *li*. *Li* in its pure essence is formless, colorless, and omnipresent in the universe. But *ki* in its operation and movement form many different phenomena. *Li* is infinite and has no limitation, but *ki* is finite and has limitations.[14]

Yulgok always strived for the unity of reality in its ultimate origin.

He aimed at the transcendence of dualism. In this respect he was different from Chu Hsi's dualism of *li* and *ki* to some extent, and from the dualism of *Yin* and *Yang (Um-yang* in Korean), the negative and positive principles of the universe. Yulgok's metaphysical concept of *li-ki* monism was applied also to his ethical concept of the unity of all. He wanted to transcend the dichotomy of self and others which was considered by him as the root of evils such as hatred and conflict.

One may question the legitimacy of Yulgok's identification of *li* and *ki,* the principle and energy, spirit and movement, essence and function, while he was at the same time maintaining the duality of them. To claim that they are two, yet they are one is irrational and ambiguous, although to some extent Yulgok's explanation is understandable. To identify *li,* which is infinite and *ki,* which in finite is illogical, although often Oriental philosophy as a whole, as in this case, transcends the ordinary logic through a mystical approach. Yulgok's mystical notion of the metaphysical, ontological, and ethical unity of *li* and *ki* is always susceptible to the critical judgment of logically and rationally oriented insights as subjectivistic and irrational idea.

Conclusion

Although Yulgok's thought had some original and unique development, it later fell into an association with political party struggles *(Tangjaeng)* in the Yi Dynasty, and it became an empty, abstract theory as the tool of politicans to argue among themselves whose interpretation of Confucianism is right or wrong. Many Confucians in the Yi Dynasty spent their time in argument of who is orthodox and who is heretic. Many of them thought that the interpretation of Chu Hsi (Chinese Neo-Confucianist) alone is correct. Under the political leadership of many idle and selfish scholars who were busy in party struggles, the nation fell into deep political and economic chaos.

Against this background, new generations of scholars arose to reform the corrupt and idle Confucianism of Korea around the Eighteenth and Nineteenth Centuries A.D. They founded *Silhak* which means "Practical Learning" or "Practical School." It may be translated as "Pragmatism." Silhak scholars opposed abstract theoretical arguments of Sŏnglihak as empty discussion and claimed that the real task of Confucianism is dealing with practical social issues, that is, to establish order in society and save people from social, political and economic troubles through the spirit of genuine human concern taught by Confucius and Mencius. The great leader of the Silhak movement was Tasan, Chŏng Yak-yong (18th–19th Century A.D.). Korean Silhak was influenced by the Western scientific and philosophical thought such as democracy which came from China primarily through Christian missionaries and Korean students who had been in China. Most Silhak scholars were Christian (Catholic) converts. Regretfully, the Silhak movement did not succeed in its objective, for when the Korean government suppressed Christianity, the Silhak movement was also swept away.[15]

Confucianism in Korea helped establish a certain level of high ethics through its educational system which emphasized the systematic training and discipline of high moral character and conduct, such as respect for parents, elders, and rulers. It shaped the general culture of the Yi Dynasty, establishing the political, social, educational, economic, and ethical system. All government officials had to pass civil service examinations based upon Confucian classics and philosophy.

But Korean Confucianism also greatly damaged the health and progress of Korea as a nation through its degeneration into party struggle and by almost absolutizing the feudal system in which the upper ruling class monopolized the wealth and power, suppressing the lower-class peasants for centuries. Confucianism also drove the Korean mentality away from independent spirit to extreme reverence for Chinese thought and culture.

Like Confucianism in China, Confucianism in Korea also could not provide the ultimate answer for the destiny of man in relation to God. Confucianism as a man-centered philosophy fundamentally lacked the ideas of God, sin, and after-life. Thus, Confucianism could not satisfy the ultimate concern of many Koreans with any lasting appeal. The man-centered philosophy thus produced party struggle to an uncontrollable degree in the political structure of the Yi Dynasty which brought the nation into political, social, and economic chaos and its ultimate collapse. The Yi Dynasty ended at the beginning of the twentieth century by the conquest of the Japanese, and it became the last dynasty in Korean history. Confucianism as the official state religion and philosophy also ended together with the end of the Yi Dynasty. Today Confucianism exists in Korea mostly in the form of ethical principles, such as filial piety and respect for elders. But these ideas are gradually fading away. Confucianism is thus a comparatively weak religion and philosophy today in Korea.

CH'ONDOGYO

Introduction

Ch'ōndogyo is the unique and relatively new religion born in Korea. It was originally called Tonghak, which means "Eastern Learning." It was founded by Ch'oe Suun (Che-u) in 1860 and was carried down through his successors such as Ch'oe Haewol (Si-hyong), Son Uiam (Byong-hi), and others to this day. The name Tonghak was changed into Ch'ōndogyo in 1905. Ch'ōndogyo means "The Religion of Heavenly Way." It is proud of its unique beliefs and achievements. The concept of man occupies the central place in the entire structure of Ch'ōndogyo thought.[16]

Man is conceived to be God, yet he is to believe in God. The immortality of the individual soul is denied, yet the eternal survival of one's character is affirmed. Ch'ōndogyo has an eschatology of humanity, yet it is limited to "the kingdom of heaven on earth." It is largely a humanistic religion, but it insists that it is not atheism.

Ch'ōndogyo as a religion in general made some of the most significant impacts upon modern Korean society. Ch'ōndogyo is the only high and mass religion originated in Korea with a strong nationalistic tendency, and yet with a broad perspective of the universal salvation of mankind. It has about 600,000 members. Over against Confucianism, Taoism, Buddhism, and Christianity, Ch'ōndogyo occupies the unique place as a new and native religion in Korea.

Ch'ōndogyo claims that its anthropology, which identifies man with God, has provided the strongest motivation towards changing the social and political pattern of Korea from a rigid feudalism to a gradual awakening to modern democracy, and has helped to bring about the fall of age-old feudalistic ethics in Korean society, for it possessed a profound revolutionary implication related to man's basic dignity and equality in society. The movement, which is considered as one of the most significant events that have changed modern Korean society was the Tonghak Revolution of 1894.

With the theme of *poguk anmin* (protecting the nation and securing peace for the people) the Ch'ŏndogyo philosophy of man has also inspired the sense of national freedom over against foreign invasions such as that from Japan. And with the theme of *tonggwi ilch'e* (all men return to unity), Ch'ŏndogyo attempts to provide an ideological basis for the national unity, especially in the divided situation of the nation between north and south. The social and political aspects of Ch'ŏndogyo are rooted in its religious philosophy of man.

The main structure of Ch'ŏndogyo philosophy may be divided into the origin of man, the nature of man, the conduct of man, the destiny of man, and the relation of Ch'ŏndogyo thought with the destiny of the nation.

The Origin of Man

Ch'ŏndogyo thinkers make a sharp distinction between their concept of the origin of man and the Christian concept. Yi Ton-hwa and Paek Semyong are the foremost Ch'ŏndogyo authors who have rejected the Christian concept of the creation of man by a transcendent and personal Creator as mythological and dualistic.[17] God in Ch'ŏndogyo is designated as *Hanul* (Heaven), or *Hanullim* or *Chŏnju* (Lord of Heaven), which virtually means God in the Western terminology. Yi Ton-hwa and others interpreted these words in philosophical terms as the Great I, or Totality, in relation to the small I, or part, which is man.[18]

Ch'ŏndogyo stresses that man is not created by a supernatural God who exists objectively outside man, but rather is caused by an immanent God, who is simply the Totality in relation to man as an individuated being. This view of Ch'ŏndogyo is monistic and pantheistic. Ch'ŏndogyo conceives that man is the eternal part of the eternal universe, and therefore, there is no way to assign a date for the origin of man.

When Ch'ŏndogyo thinkers describe the origin of man, they use the term *chohwa,* which literally means "making," or the term *muwi ihwa,* which means "natural becoming." These two terms are really equivalent in Ch'ŏndogyo.[19] These terms signify that man is a product of the self-evolution of God, and not a creation by a Creator. This concept of "muwi ihwa" was influenced by the Taoist concept of "wu-wei", which means naturalness.[20] According to Ch'ŏndogyo thinkers, man is an individuated being from the original body of life, God, and is the highest stage in the evolutionary process of God.

Ch'ŏndogyo uses also another important term, *Chigi* (ultimate energy) to denote the ultimate source of man as well as the universe.[21] *Chigi* is a monistic power immanent in the universe. It is the ultimate ground of being and the evolutionary force through which all things are manifested. Often this term is used interchangeably with the Total Life, the Original Life, the Totality, and God.

The Nature of Man

The most important and essential doctrine in Ch'ŏndogyo is *in nae Ch'ŏn,* which literally means "man is Heaven."[22] Since "Heaven" in the Far East generally means "God" in the Western language as the Absolute and Supreme Being, *in nae Ch'ŏn* may be rendered as "man is God."

Since man is an individuated life from the Total Life, God, Ch'ŏndogyo affirms logically that man is one with God in the essence of his being. Hence, *in nae Ch'ŏn* expresses the heart of the Ch'ŏndogyo concept of the nature of man. It denotes the fundamental monism of Ch'ŏndogyo in regard to man and his relation to God. Ch'ŏndogyo conceives that since man is the most highly developed being among all beings evolved from the Totality, man represents the most highly spiritual being and the very manifestation of the essence of God. On the basis of such a consideration, Ch'ŏndogyo affirms that man is God.

There is another important term which expresses the nature of man in Ch'ŏndogyo. It is *si Ch'ŏnju,* which means "man bears God" or "man serves God."[23] *Si Ch'ŏnju* signifies that man bears the essence of God within himself, or man serves God who is a Higher Spirit within man himself. Thus, there is a logical connection between *si Ch'ŏnju* and *in nae Ch'ŏn,* according to Ch'ŏndogyo. Because man bears the essence of God, he is God.

At the moment of the mystical experience, when Suun, the founder, was shaken by a sudden cold feeling, and with the feeling of the touching of the Spirit and hearing an inner voice, yet without being able to see and hear objectively, Suun asked God about the reason for his feeling. Then God said, "My mind is your mind. . . Man does not know ghost, and ghost is also I."[24] There seems to be some ambiguity at this point, that is, although being unable to hear, yet "God said" something to Suun. How could one understand what God said without being able to hear? Granted that it was a mystical experience, still ambiguity and question remain here as far as rational understanding is concerned. Of course, most Oriental philosophies and religions in such cases resort to so called "intuition" or "transcendental wisdom" as a higher level of knowledge than reason, as Ch'ōndogyo does here. And mysticism as a form of knowing experience may not be dismissed simply because it does not fit into the category of ordinary knowing experience.

Anyhow such mystical experience of Suun became the foundation of the doctrine of *in nae Ch'ōn,* for it revealed that there is no dichotomy between God and man and no dichotomy between God and ghosts. One is many, and many are one. This is the monistic perspective of reality in Ch'ōndogyo. Although the phrase *in nae Ch'ōn* was coined by Son Uiam, the third leader of Ch'ōndogyo,[25] the idea of man's essential oneness with God was already established in the thought and experience of Suun, the founder.

Haewol, the second leader of Ch'ōndogyo, has also stressed man's essential oneness with God, and many of his expressions have undoubtedly become the basis of Uiam's phrase of *in nae Ch'ōn,* Haewol stated the concept as follows:

> Man is a lump of Heaven, and Heaven is the Spirit
> of all things.
> Man is Heaven, and Heaven is man.
> Outside man, there is no Heaven,
> and outside Heaven, there is no man.[26]

The statement here sounds confusing and irrational, but it denotes the pantheistic monism of Ch'ōndogyo, which sees all things as ultimately one. Haewol also used the phrase, *in si Ch'ōn,* which also literally means "man is Heaven" just like Uiam's phrase, *in nae Ch'ōn.*

Logically speaking, if man is God, then there would be no God outside man as the object of faith. Ch'ōndogyo claims, however, that it is not an atheism, but rather it represents the true and right faith. According to Ch'ŏndogyo, one should believe in God, who is not in a distant place, but within oneself as the immanent reality.

In a more radical way, a Ch'ŏndogyo leader explains that nature of *in nae Ch'ŏn* faith as "I believing me."[27] This means that the small I is ultimately concerned about the great I; I as man is serving I as God.[28] Thus, this conception indicates that faith in Ch'ŏndogyo is a humanistic faith.

Concerning the soul and body relationships, Ch'ŏndogyo recognizes the difference between soul and body in man, but it always emphasizes the unity between the two. Man is conceived as one person, and body and soul are simply two aspects of one human being. Ch'ŏndogyo denies the immortality of an individual soul as an entity, but it affirms the immortality of personality *(in gyok),* that is, the character of a person.[29]

Concerning good and evil in human nature, Ch'ŏndogyo conceives that man's original nature is free from evil.[30] This is similar to Mencius' *Song son sol* (theory of good nature).[31] Evil in human nature is considered as *a posteriori* product.

The Conduct of Man (Ethics)

The unique principle of human conduct in Ch'ŏndogyo is called *sain yŏch'on,* which means "treat man as God."[32] This ethical idea is based on the ideas of *si Ch'ŏnju* and *in nae Ch'ŏn.* Since the nature of man is divine, it follows logically that man ought to be treated as God. Along with this central idea, there are other minor concepts such as *kunja (chun-tzu* in Chinese) which means superior man, and *tok (te* in Chinese) which means virtue.[33] In some of such ideas, we find an obvious influence of Confucianism on Ch'ŏndogyo ethics.[34]

Since the early beginning stage, Ch'ŏndogyo has laid a strong emphasis on equality and justice in human society. It proclaimed equality between the yangban (the aristocrat) and ssangnom (the vulgar), and between the legitimate and illegitimate sons.[35] It also regarded women as equal to men. Imagine what kind of reaction such democratic equalitarian social ideas could have caused in the rigid feudalistic society of 19th Century Korea. Its strong opposition to the social discrimination between the aristocratic class and commoner class and between the legitimate and illegitimate children was revolutionary in that age, although Ch'ŏndogyo was probably not the only voice of challenge to the age-old discriminatory tradition of the time, for there were already deep-seated complaints among many Koreans at that time as well as the external influences reaching the Land of Morning Calm through the wind of democratic ideas brought by Western missionaries.

One of the strong reasons why Ch'ŏndogyo emphasized the democratic ideas of equality and justice is probably that most of the early leaders of Ch'ŏndogyo were born and raised in relatively poor families and experienced personally the bitter taste of social discrimination in their lives. Suun, the founder, was a soja, an illegitimate son, although one of his ancestors was a very famous yangban scholar in Silla Kingdom. Hence, as a soja, Suun was prohibited from any chance to rise to any high position in the socio-political system of the time. The combination of personal disappointment and deteriorating social conditions of the time, which Suun termed as "sickness," were probably the main causes of Suun's search for the way-out and subsequent establishment of a movement called Tonghak.

The like-minded disillusioned masses flocked into Suun's teaching of so-called "salvation," and the movement quickly spread wide to many corners of the nation. The democratic idea of equality of all men regardless of the social class background must have had a great appeal to those oppressed masses, and this is probably the reason why the Ch'ŏndogyo as a movement was highly successful in its early stage. Soon the movement born under the loosely formulated ideas refined its ideas and expanded more. Under the banner of *in nae Ch'ŏn* and *sain yŏch'on* the movement became so large and powerful, when it challenged the government forces in 1894 that they alone could not subdue the Tonghak forces. Only through the help of the Japanese and Chinese forces could they defeat the so-called Tonghak Rebellion.

It is a well known fact among historians that the Tonghak Rebellion was the main cause of the Sino-Japanese War, the fall of the Yi Dynasty, the end of the imperial system of Korea, the Japanese colonialism in Korea, and ultimately the dawn of modernization of Korea in the areas of social class system, education, and culture in general.[36]

The Destiny of Man (Eschatology)

Ch'ŏndogyo as a religion teaches salvation. Individually, salvation means the re-creation of personality. According to Ch'ŏndogyo, many people in the world have "sickness" in their nature, nct living according to the principles of respect and faithfulness to their moral duties. The "sickness" can be healed through improving one's character.[37] Hence, the Ch'ŏndogyo concept of salvation is basically ethical and humanistic. Therefore, the ideas of heaven and hell beyond this world are absent in Ch'ŏndogyo thought.[38]

However, Ch'ŏndogyo uses the phrase, "the eternal life of manhood."[39] It means that man's character can live on eternally in the memory of humanity, especially in his descendants, when he lives a good moral life.[40]

As the method of achieving salvation, Ch'ŏndogyo prescribes certain religious training such as meditation, service, and certain other rules of practice. But essentially the method seems to be mental and ethical training.

Concerning the social dimension of human destiny, Ch'ŏndogyo advocates from its early days the slogan of *poguk anmin,* "protecting the nation and securing peace for the people."[41] Since the days of Suun, and through most periods of Ch'ŏndogyo history, Korea as a nation and people suffered insecurity and pains through the internal ill conditions as well as the brutal threat and harms from foreign powers. Thus, Ch'ŏndogyo often stood in the front line opposing these evil forces and fought for the salvation of the nation. The Samil Independence Movement of 1919 is the great example, in which Ch'ŏndogyo played the leading role among the religious groups in Korea in terms of leadership and financing the movement.

Ch'ŏndogyo also teaches the idea of "the kingdom of heaven on earth," which is the ultimate goal in Ch'ŏndogyo thought.[42] The kingdom of heaven is not somewhere outside or beyond this world, but it must be realized in this world. When all evil forces and sickness cease to exist, it can be realized, according to Ch'ŏndogyo. Again here we find that Ch'ŏndogyo eschatology is basically this-worldly and humanistic.

One of the central ideas of Ch'ŏndogyo eschatology is *tonggwi ilch'e,* which means "all men will return to unity."[43] It means that all men and especially Koreans among themselves will be united ultimately through understanding and cooperation to achieve harmony and peace.

Ch'ondogyo Thought and its Relation to the Political Situation in North and South Korea

Since the division of Korea in 1945, Ch'ŏndogyo, like other religions, suffered considerably, losing its membership in North Korea, where religious freedom is suppressed to the maximum extent, if not completely. There was a large number of Ch'ŏndogyoists in North Korea before 1945. There may be very few Ch'ŏndogyoists today in North Korea.

The Ch'ŏndogyo political party has been known as Ch'ŏngudang (Young Friends' Party) in North Korea. Even today it exists in North Korea, but its role is not at all significant. In North Korea the strongest political party is Chosŏn Nodongdang (Korean Workers' Party), which has virtual monopoly of party power. Other parties are allowed to function only for propaganda purposes to appear to other nations as if there is a religious and political freedom in North Korea. Another party, beside Ch'ŏngudang, which has the function of a nominal figure, is Chomindang founded by Cho Mansik.

For purely propaganda purposes in the international community North Korea has been preaching the so-called democratic frontier for the unification of motherland and claimed that all political parties are permitted. But in reality all the parties do not have the equal competitive function, but rather complementary function to Nodongdang. Playing the role of nominal figure, Ch'ŏngudang has been headed by Kim Byong-che, Kim Tal-hyon, and presently by Park Sin-t'ak.[44]

Nevertheless, in rural areas Ch'ŏngudang had a strong following among the peasants before the Korean War in 1950. When the U.N. forces captured North Korea during the Korean War, Ch'ŏngudang organized the anti-Communits forces and aided the U.N. forces. But when the U.N. forces retreated to the South, the North Korean Communists began to persecute the Ch'ŏngudang severely. Since then, Ch'ŏngudang has been weakened greatly, and it barely exists nominally for the propaganda value of North Korea.

Ch'ŏndogyo in South Korea does not have any political party. Its main function in South Korea is religion. In South Korea which has a democratic form of government, Ch'ŏndogyo as well as other religions enjoys religious freedom. The South Korean government as well as all religions in South Korea seems to take for granted that there is a clear separation between religion and politics. Thus, at present, there is no religious political party. Ch'ŏndogyo in South Korea does not seem to have any intention to organize a political party at the present moment. However, when we consider that there is a highly active political party in Japan which is based on Sokagakai (a modern Japanese Buddhist sect) philosophy and its financial and voting power, no one may say that such a movement is imposssible with Ch'ŏndogyo in Korea.

At present in South Korea Ch'ŏndogyo has a strong anti-Communist and pro-democratic standpoint. Many of the present Ch'ŏndogyo leaders voice such attitudes through their writings. Especially this is true when we consider the opinion of the present head (Kyoryŏng) of Ch'ŏndogyo, Ch'oe Tŏk-sin, who is a retired general of the Korean Military Forces and a former ambassador of South Korea to West Germany.[45] Ch'ŏndogyo considers that it, as a religious and spiritual movement, is incompatible with communism, which is atheistic materialism.

Ch'ŏndogyo has a strong concern for the destiny of the nation. It has made a great effort to bring about the well-being of the nation for a long time, especially when the nation was suffering under the discriminatory socio-economic-political system of feudalism, when the nation was suffering under Japanese colonialism, and again at the present time when the nation is suffering under the divided condition between the North and South. Ch'ŏndogyo, through its doctrines of *poguk anmin* (protecting the nation and securing peace for the people) and *tonggwi ilch'e* (all men will return to unity), makes every effort to provide a strong philosophical basis for the unification of the tragically divided nation.

Concluding Remarks

There are some elements inherently dynamic in the Ch'ŏndogyo philosophy of man which motivated the oppressed masses of the feudalistic society of the 19th Century Korea to challenge the existing discriminatory and oppressive system. Certainly no one can ignore the significant impact of Ch'ōndogyo as a movement upon modern Korean society. But regarding the extent of the impact, there may be no exact agreement between the Ch'ōndogyo thinkers and many non-Ch'ōndogyo historians.

The impact of the Ch'ōndogyo philosophy of man on Korean society might have been once significant through its democratic ideas of equality and justice in the feudalistic age, but its impact at present and in the future seems somewhat doubtful, since Korean society has already become democratic to a great extent, if not completely. However, through the revitalization and strengthening of their philosophical ideas, such as *poguk anmin* and *tonggwi ilch'e,* Ch'ōndogyo may further be able to contribute to the national unification in the future. Whether or not Ch'ōndogyo will grow further and remain strong in Korea remains to be seen. Perhaps, for the reason that Ch'ōndogyo is the only major "Korean" religion born in the native land, and in the name of its uniqueness, it may still have a chance to attract the attention of Koreans as well as foreigners.

But in Ch'ōndogyo thought there are some inherent weaknesses. Man is identified with God, yet man is to serve God. This notion involves a logical contradiction. Such a deification of man is a great sin in Judeo-Christian thought. The Ch'ōndogyo notion of man's achievement of his own salvation and realization of the Kingdom of Heaven on earth through man's self-effort characterizes Ch'ōndogyo as a man-centered philosophy.

FOOTNOTES

[1]Cf. Kim Tōk-hwang, *Han'guk Ssangsa* (A History of Korean Thought) (Seoul: Namsandang, 1963), pp. 26-27.

[2]*Ibid.,* pp. 25-26.

[3]Cf. Kim Tōk-hwang, *Han'guk Chonggyosa* (A History of Korean Religions) (Seoul: Haemunsa, 1963), pp. 41-42.

[4]Tongshik Ryu, *Han'guk Chonggyowa Kidoggyo* (The Christian Faith Encounters The Religions of Korea) (Seoul: The Christian Literature Society of Korea, 1965), p. 18.

[5]*Ibid.;* Cf. *Han'guk Sasangsa,* pp. 25ff.

[6]Chosōn is the name of ancient Korea, which means the Land of Morning

Calm. Japanese used to call Korea by this name, and North Korea calls itself often as Chosōn.

[7]Han U-kūn, *Kuksa* (The National History) (Seoul: Suhomyon'gusa, 1955), pp. 4-5; An Ho-sang, *Paedalui Chonggyowa Ch'orhakgwa Yoksa* (Religion, Philosophy, and History of Korea) (Seoul: Omun'gak, 1959), pp. 25ff.

[8]Han, p. 4.

[9]*Han'guk Chonggyosa*, pp. 97ff.

[10]*Ibid.*, pp. 115-117; Ryu, p. 46.

[11]Rhi Ki-young, *Wonhyo Sasang* (Wonhyo's Thought), Vol. I, (Seoul: Woneumkak, 1967), pp. 3ff.

[12]Ryu, pp. 50f.

[13]Hyon Sang-yun, *Chosōn Yuhaksa* (A History of Korea Confucianism) (Seoul: Minjungsogwan, 1954), p. 114. *Li* may be translated as principle or idea, and *ki* may be translated as energy or air. There is an interesting similarity between these concepts and the Platonic concept of Idea (Form) and Matter.

[14]*Ibid.; Han'guk Sasangsa*, pp. 134-135.

[15]Han, pp. 150ff.

[16]See Yong Choon Kim, "The Concept of Man in Ch'ondogyo." (Unpublished Ph.D. Dissertation, Temple University, 1969). Some eminent Korean scholars, such as Yi Sōn-gūn, President of Yongnam University, and Ch'oe Tong-hui, Professor at Korea University, consider Ch'ondogyo thought very highly. See Yi's article, "Tonghak Undong kwa Han'guk ui Kundaehwa Kwajong" (Tonghak Movement and the Process of Modernization of Korea), *Han'guk Sasang* (Korean Thought) IV (1962), 14-28; Ch'oe's article, "Suun ui In'gan Kwan" (Suun's Concept of Man), *Korean Thought*, I and II (1959), 86-95.

[17]Yi Ton-hwa, *Sinin Ch'orhak* (Philosophy of New Man) (Seoul: Ilsinsa, 1963), pp. 15ff.; Paek Se-myong, *Tonghak Sasang kwa Ch'ondogyo* (Tonghak Thought and Ch'ondogyo) (Seoul: Tonghaksa, 1956), p. 42.

[18]Yi Ton-hwa, pp. 9-10.

[19]Ch'oe Suun, "Nonhangmun" (Writing on Discussion and Learning), *Ch'ondogyo Kyōngjōn* (Ch'ondogyo Scripture) (Seoul: Ch'ondogyo Central HQ, 1961), p. 13; Yi Ton-hwa, pp. 11ff. and pp. 37ff.; Peak, pp. 46ff.

[20]Lao Tzu, *Tao Te Ching*, the original text in Kim Kyong-t'ak, *Lao Tzu* (Seoul: Kwangmun Ch'ulpansa, 1965), Chaps. 2, 37, 38, 43, 48, 57 and 63.; Cf. Yi Ton-hwa, *In Nae Ch'on Youi* (The Essential Meaning of 'Man is God') (Seoul: Ch'ondogyo Central HQ, 1968), pp. 81-82; 128ff.

[21]Han T'ae-yon, *Ch'ōndo Sipsam Kang* (Thirteen Lectures on the Heavenly Way) (Seoul: Yōngjin Munhwasa, 1967), p. 143; *Ch'ōndogyo Kyōngjōn*, p. 32.

[22]*In Nae Ch'ōn Youi*, p. 24; Han Tae-yon, p. 54; Pack, p. 53.

[23]"Nonhangmun," *Ch'ōndogyo Kyōngjōn*, p. 13; Pack, Se-myong, *Tonghak Kyōngjōn Haeui* (An Interpretation of Tonghak Scripture) (Seoul: Han'guk Sasang Yon'guhoe, 1963), p. 80.

[24]"Nonhangmun," *Ch'ōndogyo Kyōngjōn*, p. 9.

[25]Son Uiam, "Sōngnyōng Ch'ulsesōl" (The Doctrine of the Transmigration of the Spirit), *Ch'ōndogyo Kyōngjōn*, p. 358.

[26]Ch'oe Haewol, "Ch'ōn, In, Kwisin, Ūmyang" (Heaven, Man, Spirit, and Yin-Yang), *Ch'ōndogyo Kyōngjōn*, p. 142.

[27]Pak Ūng-sam, "Ch'ōndogyo ui Parun Sinang) (The Right Faith of Ch'ōn-

dogyo), *Sinin'gan* (New Humanity), XXIX (December, 1963), 21.

[28]*Ibid.,* p. 22.

[29]*Tonghak Sasang kwa Ch'ŏndogyo,* pp. 63ff.

[30]*Ibid.,* pp. 118ff.

[31]Mencius, *Mencius,* the original text in Kim Kyong-t'ak, *Mencius and Chungyong* (Seoul: Kwangmun Ch'ulp'ansa, 1965), Pt. VI, Ch. 11, "Koja P'yon" A, Sec. 2, p. 405.

[32]*Tonghak Sasang kwa Ch'ŏndogyo,* p. 60.

[33]"Nonhangmun," *Ch'ŏndogyo Kyŏngjŏn,* pp. 13-14.

[34]For *chun-tzu* see Suun, "Podŏngmun" (Writing on Spreading Virtue), *Ch'ŏndogyo Kyŏngjŏn,* p. 2; "Todōkka" (Song of Morality), *Ch'ŏndogyo Kyŏngjŏn,* pp. 116-118; for *te see Ibid.;* Cf. Confucius, *Lun Yu* (The Analects), the original text in Kim Kyong-t'ak, *Lun Yu* and *Ta Hsueh* (Seoul: Kwangmun Ch'ulp'ansa, 1965), I, 1, 8, 14; II, 12-14; IV, 5, 6, *(chun-tzu);* II, 1; IV, 25 *(te).*

[35]Yi Ton-hwa, *Suun Simbōp Kangui* (Lecture on Suun's Theory on Mind) (Seoul: Ch'ŏndogyo Central HQ, 1968), p. 132; Han U-gūn, *Kuksa* (National History), Seoul: Suhom Yon'gusa, 1955), pp. 109-110; Ch'oe Haewol, "Nanui Nundap" (Question and Answer on the Difficult Problems), *Ch'ŏndogyo Kyŏngjŏn,* pp. 219-219.

[36]See Han U-gūn, pp. 173ff.; Kim Sang-gi, "Kabo Tonghak Undong ui Yoksajok Uiui" (The Historical Significance of the Tonghak Movement of 1894), *Han'guk Sasang,* I and II, 36-41; *Tonghak Sasang kwa Ch'ŏndogyo,* p. 141.

[37]"P'odongmun," *Ch'ŏndogyo Kyŏngjŏn,* p. 4; *Tonghak Sasang kwa Ch'ondogyo,* p. 83.

[38]*Ibid.,* pp. 160ff.

[39]*Ibid.,* p. 88.

[40]*Ibid.,* p. 106.

[41]"P'odongmun," *Ch'ŏndogyo Kyŏngjŏn,* pp. 3ff.

[42]Han T'ae-yon, pp. 79-81.

[43]*Ibid.,* pp. 156-157; Pak Ung-sam, "Tonggwi Ilch'e" (All Men Return to Unity), *Sinin'gan,* XVI (December, 1959), 64-69.

[44]Ku Hon-hwoe, "Kōpbyōnhanūn Kukjejōngsewa Hangukui Anbo Munje" (Quickly Changing International Political Situation and the Problem of the Security of Korea), *Sinin'gan,* Vol. 289 (September, 1971), p. 67.

[45]Ch'oe Tōk-sin, "T'ongile Taebihanun Kungminui Chase" (The Attitude of the Nation in Preparation for Unification), *Sinin'gan,* Vol. 290 (October, 1971), pp. 9ff.; Paek Se-myong, *Hanaro Kanūnkil* (Road to Oneness) (Seoul: Ilsinsa, 1968), pp. 46ff.; Mun Che-kyong, "Ch'ondogyoui Pankong Undong (Pukhan)" (The Anti-Communist Movement of Ch'ondogyo: North Korea), *Sinin'gan,* Vol. 288 (August, 1971), pp. 85ff.

CHAPTER VII

JAPANESE THOUGHT

JAPANESE THOUGHT from its early period has been influenced by Shinto mythology. Later, Buddhism and Confucianism joined in shaping Japanese thought. More recently, the whole of Japanese thought is undergoing a dramatic change due to the influence of Western culture, mainly the influence of Western political, social, and economic thought. Religiously and philosophically, the Japanese still maintain a considerable amount of uniqueness, which is the heritage from Japan's past.

The beginning of Japanese culture is much later than that of China and Korea. Little is known of the early Japanese history and culture prior to the Christian era. The early history of Japan is based on legend and mythology.[1] Probably the Yamato clan, which became the ruling clan in Japan, as well as most Japanese, came from a Mongoloid race in the continent. The development of Japanese culture in its early stage was much dependent upon the influence of Chinese and Korean cultures. Although Buddhism and Confucianism of Japan are very much similar to those of China and Korea, there are some differences mainly due to the Japanization of the originally foreign elements. Such cultural assimilation and transformation are not unique to Japan.

SHINTO

Introduction

Shinto is an indigenous and unique religion in Japan. It is the nationalistc ideology of the Japanese people. Shinto literally means "the way of gods." It has no founder and no official scriptures. From the prehistoric past Shinto seems to have been the major ideological basis of the Japanese people. It has been the unique way of life for the majority of the Japanese. But in its development it has been influenced by many foreign ideas.

The distinctive symbols of Shinto are *tori* and shrine. *Tori* is the gateway to a shrine, which symbolically divides the sacred and the secular. Shinto shrines have a rather unique architectural shape as a symbol of Shinto. The Shinto shrines are simple in design and decoration, usually nothing more than a thatched roof supported by straight pillars. Within them there is a symbolic representation of deity, a substitute spirit which might be a stone or a mirror. Ordinarily there are no images in a Shinto shrine. Shintoists put straw ropes around shrines and white papers on ropes. These are designed to mark off the sacred place and to protect the object of worship from evil influences. Inside the shrines there are short sticks with paper strips. These are symbolic offerings and occasionally are regarded as symbols of gods. Near the shrine, there is usually fresh water, a spring or a basin, for the purification of the worshippers.[2]

The two most important ideas of Shinto are the notions of *kami* (gods), which is basically polytheism and animism, and the idea of emperor-worship, which was a means of unifying the nation. The Shinto idea of god shows the primitive nature of its belief. Shinto is sometimes called a religion of nature worship, for nature is regarded as the abode of the deities. Shintoists worship the spirit of trees, mountains, rocks, and seas. They also worship deified ancestors and heroes, as well as emperors.

Shinto is sometimes known as an ultranationalistic religion which made the Japanese people an emperor-worshipping nation. State Shinto, a religious system supported by the government for its nationalistic goal, was abolished at the end of the Second World War. But Sectarian Shinto still remains a major religion in Japan. There are many types of Shinto at present. The essential beliefs of modern Shinto are rooted in primitive Shinto.

Primitive Shinto

The early Japanese did not have a systematic philosophical thought with respect to the nature of the world, man, and god. They had relatively simple, vague, and mythological ideas concerning them. Shinto, as the early religion of the Japanese people, often meant the magico-religious beliefs and practices of the Japanese derived from gods.[3]

According to Kitagawa, the main characteristic of early Shinto was the notion of *kami,* which is usually translated as gods, spirits, and sometimes as "above," "superior," or "numinous or sacred nature."[4] Kitagawa explains the essential idea of early Shinto as follows:

> While early Shinto was not interested in speculating on the meta-physical meaning of the world, the early Japanese took it for granted that they were integrally part of the cosmos, which they saw as a "community of living beings," all sharing the kami (sacred) nature. The Japanese myths mention the existence of eight hundred myriads of kami, a metaphor employed to express belief in the sacredness of the whole universe. In such a world view, people did not consider them-selves in any way separated from cosmic existence and the rhythm of nature.[5]

The early Japanese felt a profound kinship with the world of nature. They felt that they were part and instruments of the kami in nature. Their self-understanding was always in relation to the kami. Early Shintoists believed in many gods.

> They believed that all natural phenomena were of animistic character and that each person or thing was in itself a manifestation of the divine. Though all things were thought individually to possess a spirit, there was no conception of an immortal soul and no philosophical speculation on life and death. The anthropomorphic concept of deities no doubt existed, as evidenced by legends and myths about the creation of the universe, but the deities of the primitive Japanese pantheon were not well defined, and their powers and characters were very nebulous. Anything which evoked a feeling of awe was reversed as being particularly imbued with divine or mysterious power; therefore, the forces of nature, especially awe-inspiring trees, rocks, or mountains, and other inex-plicable natural phenomena became objects of worship. They were given the name *kami.*[6]

The early religion of Japan included primitive forms of rituals such as sorcery, divination, purification rites, and thanksgiving for harvests and the favors of nature. Among many deities they revered and worshipped were clan chieftains and the spirits of dead ancestors.[7]

According to Kitagawa, there were two characteristics of early Shinto. First, early Shinto stressed a sense of gratitude toward the *kami.* Occasionally there were sorrows and a feeling of fear toward evil *kami,* but on the whole, life was good and beautiful, and men were grateful to the *kami* for the life they enjoyed in this world. Second, early Shinto emphasized purification. The early Japanese were not concerned with moral sins but physical and mental defilements, which early Shinto taught to cleanse ceremonially by exorcism and abstention. Early Shinto had terms of sin and evil, but it did not consider them as reality. It regarded them as a lack of harmony and beauty and believed that they could be corrected through purification rituals.[8]

In early Shinto mythology we find a three-dimensional universe. First, the highest realm called "The Plain of the High Sky" is where male and female kami reside. Second, the lowest region called "The Nether World" is where unclean and evil spirits reside. Third, the middle world called "The Manifested World" is where men and other animals reside. However, the early Japanese had a vague notion of the difference between the three dimensions of the universe. They referred to both the heavenly realm and the nether world as being in the "other world," which was sometimes associated with certain mountains or islands believed to exist beyond the sea.[9]

The early Japanese believed in all kinds of kami, benevolent and malevolent, strong and weak. They thought that some kami have power and authority to rule, others bring about union and harmony, others cause miseries, and others impart blessings. Sometimes spirits of animals were venerated.[10]

As Japan progressed toward a unified nation, changes took place in Japanese religious ideas. Early Shinto lacked fixed liturgies and ecclesiastical organizations. Most religious exercises took place in the home, around sacred trees, sacred rocks, or in the paddy fields. There was no name for an individual kami. Kami were related usually to a particular region where one is born. Kami were regarded as the spirits who bless and protect the region in which one is born. In the farming and fishing villages, which were the majority of communities in the pre-modern Japan, the kami of agriculture and those of the sea were worshipped according to the proper seasons.[11]

Tennoism

Among many types of Shinto, Tennoism is most interesting. Tennoism means belief in the emperor *(tenno)* as god and as the manifestation of the Absolute on the basis that he is the direct descendant of the Sun Goddess. Emperor worship is one of the oldest traditions of Shinto, and according to the legend of the Japanese people, the Yamato clan became dominant among all the clans of early Japan; the legend of the Yamato clan eventually became the national legend. In early Japan, the emperor was both the ruler and the chief priest of the nation. He became the chief intermediary between the people and the Sun Goddess. According to Shinto mythology, the emperor was the direct descendant of the deities who created Japan and the universe. Tennoism was also strengthened by the Confucian idea of loyalty to the emperor.[12]

Nihongi (The Chronicle of Japan) and *Kojiki* (The Record of Ancient Events) provide the information concerning the early legend and mythology of the imperial family of Japan and the creation of the islands of Japan. They are the records of the Eighth Century A.D., but they are regarded as the earliest writings of the Japanese which inform us of the development of the Japanese nation. They are regarded as sacred by Shintoists and the imperial house of Japan. They contain the account of the mythological development of Japan, and glorify Japan and its people as a superior nation. For this reason, Shinto is a very nationalistic ideology and thus quite unacceptable to other nations.

According to the *Nihongi* and *Kojiki,* the first legendary emperor ruled Japan in the Seventh Century B.C. But historians today consider that the historic period of Japan started about the Third or Fourth Century A.D.

As Japan was being unified by an imperial family, the increasing systematization of religious myths and rituals took place, and the idea of nationl kami which was orginally the kami of the imperial clan developed.

The world view represented in *Nihongi* and *Kojiki* is mythological. The central idea in them is the establishment of the divine imperial house. According to mythology, Izanagi (male kami who invites) and

Izanami (female kami who is invited) created Japan as the most beautiful place in the world.[13] They had children, such as the kami of the wind, of the tree, of the mountain, of the plains, and of the fire. Among them Amaterasu Omigami (the Sun Goddess) was most beautiful and well-behaved.[14] Thus, she was sent to rule the sun. Amaterasu Omigami became the highest deity among the Shinto pantheon, and she is the protector of Japan as a nation and people. Jimmu Tenno, the grandson of the Sun Goddess, became the first emperor of Japan, and the emperors of Japan were the direct descendants of Jimmu Tenno and thus of the Sun Goddess. On this basis Shinto established the mythological theory that emperors are divine, that Japan is a divine nation, and the Japanese are a divine and superior people.[15] This ideology was probably invented to rival the glory and power of China and to glorify the nation and the ruler of Japan; it was applied during the Second World War against the Western nations, especially the United States.

In some periods of Japanese history, the cult of emperor worship declined. But since the Meiji Restoration in 1868 in which the full and absolute authority of the emperor was restored from the hands of the Tokugawa Shogunate (military dictators), under whom the emperors had been mere figureheads for several centuries, emperor whorship was revived. After the Meiji Restoration, the imperial constitution of Japan declared that the emperor was sacred and infallible. The founders of the new Japan, which started with the Meiji Reform, manufactured a more emphatic legend or mythology of the divinity of the emperor and the superiority of Japan as a nation and people on the basis of the early Shinto mythology. They moulded the minds of the people according to their wish and design. Their purpose was the establishment of a strong unified nation under the sovereign power of the emperor based on the worship of the Sun Goddess and the emperor.

Tennoism is also called *Kokutai Shinto,* which means "the Shinto of national structure." It means that emperor worship became the fundamental principle and central ideology of the new "national structure" of Japan, especialy since the Meiji Restoration until the end of the Second World War. Emperor worship was taught as the highest morality in Japanese schools before 1945, the year when Japan lost the war.[16]

Tennoism was often taken by some people to an extreme degree. The imperial government of Japan, especially during the Second World War, required the people of Japan to pay absolute loyalty to the emperor. Japanese soldiers in the war fought and died in the name of *tenno* (the emperor) rather than in the name of the nation. At some point, many Shintoists believed that the Japanese emperor was not only the head of Japan but also the rightful ruler of the entire world. This idea became the official philosophy of the Japanese government, and it was taught in Japanese schools during the Second World War.

The aspect of the Shinto mythology which glorifies the superiority of the Japanese and their emperor as god became a very dangerous philosophy, which provided a motivating cause for the Second World War. During the war, Shinto was the state religion of Japan. The Japanese and even the Koreans and Chinese who were under the Japanese colonial rule were forced to worship the emperor and the Sun Goddess. Thousands of Christians, especially in Korea, who refused to cooperate with the Japanese government policy concerning the worship of the emperor and the Sun Goddess, were severely and cruelly persecuted in prison, and in many other ways; some were martyred. Immediately after the war, under the direction of General MacArthur, Japan adopted a democratic form of government, the emperor renounced his divinity, State Shinto was abolished, and Shinto now remains as a sectarian religion.

Household Shinto

Household Shinto is concerned with family matters, especially the celebration of birth and the anniversaries of the death of ancestors. Shinto families place a miniature shrine called *kamidana,* which literally means "god-shelf," in the living room usually above a closet. It serves as a family altar. They place sacred tablets in it.

The earnest Shintoist would rise in the morning, perform his purification ceremony, bow before the shrine, clap his hands twice, bow for a moment in silence, and then start his daily activities.[17]

Special occasions, such as the naming of a child on the seventh day after birth and the visits to the shrine on a certain ceremonial day, would be announced in front of the *kamidana.* Sometimes a priest is invited to commemorate the anniversary of the death of some ancestor. Ritual prayers are chanted and a feast is enjoyed. If there is no priest, the head of the household performs the ceremony.[18]

The Japanese government encouraged Household Shinto, especially during the Second World War. According to government policy, Household Shinto was an essential part of cultivating and strengthening Shinto as a whole. The Japanese government believed that Household Shinto was vitally important for the unity of the nation and the strengthening of the national spirit in time of trouble. Today, since the democratic consitution of the Japanese government provides the clear separation between state and religion, and since the people are no longer forced to practice Shinto, only the earnest Shintoists practice Household Shinto. These earnest Shintoists would probably account for less than half of the Japanese population. Another reason why Shinto, as well as most other religions, is declining is that many educated youth of Japan find many obviously mythological, superstitious, and irrational elements in Shinto beliefs; therefore, they are gradually turning away from Shinto traditions.

BUDDHISM IN JAPAN

Introduction

Buddhism in Japan is essentially similar to Buddhism in China and Korea, from which it came. Buddhism in East Asia, that is, Buddhism in Tibet, China, Korea, and Japan constitutes Mahayana or Northern Buddhism. Buddhism arrived in Japan from Korea around the sixth century A.D. About this time Confucianism and Taoism also came to Japan from Korea. Korean monks from the Silla Kingdom and Paekche Kingdom brought a new and higher culture to Japan, which was still a relatively primitive nation at that time.[19]

Buddhism in Japan was complimentary to Shinto beliefs in many ways. While the average Japanese went to Shinto shrines for the celebration of the birth and blessings of children, they went to Buddhist temples for assurance in paradise. Shinto lacked a well-defined theology or eschatology. Buddhism on the other hand promised to the masses paradise beyond earthly existence.

The Buddhism which was introduced into Japan contained philosophical modifications and theistic accretions and rituals totally unknown to primitive Buddhism. These fundamentally changed its original character in several important respects.

While it is impossible to determine its exact nature, the Buddhism which was first introduced into Japan contained Confucian doctrines on practical ethics, traces of Taoist dualism, and an elaborate pantheon of deities. In short, Buddhism through the centuries had absorbed so many foreign philosophies and had split into so many schools and sects that it in no way represented a unified body of religious opinion. Since Japan fell heir from the very beginning to these often-contradictory sectarian differences, it is little wonder that Japanese Buddhism never resembled the religion of the original Buddha.[20]

The Japanese modified Buddhism to a great extent and adapted it to the Japanese culture, and some Buddhist schools developed in Japan are quite different from the Buddhism of both China and Korea.[21] The Japanese schools of Tendai Buddhism, Shingon Buddhism, Amidaism and Zen Buddhism were somewhat different from the parent schools on the continent, and especially Nichirenism had some distinctively Japanese color.[22]

Pure Buddhism has practically no theology; it is basically a philosophy and must be so studied. Even as a philosophy, there is no uniformity or common pattern. Japanese Buddhism is a conglomerate of so many conflicting systems that it is as confusing as contemporary Christianity, with its Coptic, Greek Orthodox, Roman Catholic, and Protestant churches. There are, however, some elements common to the teachings of most sects, such as acceptance of S'akyamuni Gautama as the founder of Buddhism, acknowledgement of his teachings as the essence of truth, conception of the attainment of Buddhahood as salvation, belief in the "three precious things"—Buddha, the law, and the church —which S'akyamuni handed down to his followers, and belief in the three basic paths—morality, meditation, and intuition—as the proper approach to truth.[23]

However, different Buddhist schools usually have different interpretations. For example, some Buddhists believe in the mythical Buddha Amida, while others do not believe in him. There are all sorts of sectarian interpretations, speculations, and rituals, according to different schools. Early Buddhism in Japan was relatively simple, and there was no sectarian differentiation in Japanese Buddhism until the Seventh Century. The early Japanese Buddhism employed Chinese architecture, costumes, rites, and languages.

Tendai Buddhism

After the capitol was moved from Nara to Kyoto in 794 A.D.,
Saicho (767–822) known also as Dengyo Daishi, founded Tendai
Buddhism on Mount Hiei. Tendai Buddhism was eclectic. It embraced most of the contradictory sectarian beliefs of Chinese Buddhism and it left the choice of salvation to the individual. Its beliefs
included esoteric mysteries, contemplation, and faith in Amida
Buddha. Saicho attempted to synthesize all Mahayana doctrines and
taught universal salvation. But essentially Tendai emphasized that the
supreme truth can be realized only through meditation. Tendai considers the Lotus Sutra as the greatest of all Buddhist scriptures.

> The Lotus Sutra interprets the person of Buddha as a manifestation
> of metaphysical entity and synthesizes the two aspects of his being: his
> incarnation in human life and his real ontological identity. By extension,
> this conception of Buddha can be applied to the relationship between
> individual and universal existence. The Tendai philosopher observes
> that the whole and all its parts are identical, that the whole' cosmos
> is present in the minutest particle. The Tendai doctrine of ontology is
> an abstruse consideration of three forms of existence: the void, the
> temporary, and the middle. Existence or non-existence is dependent on
> relationship to the "middle," which is absolute existence. Tendai calls
> these three forms of existence the "three truths," and teaches that, when
> these truths are seen in perfect relationship, one has attained the en-
> lightenment of Buddha himself. This enlightenment must be reached
> through philosophical, training and contemplation.[24]

The essence of Tendai ethics is to live the life of the universal self.
Tendai teaches that one attains moral perfection through meditation,
faith, and initiation into a mystery. One must remove illusion to
attain perfection. Tendai Buddhism popularized Buddhism through
attempts to identify Shinto deities with those of the Buddhist pantheon,
and it played a significant role in the cultural development of Japan.
Tendai Buddhism was strong during the Ninth and Tenth Centuries.
But in the Eleventh and Twelfth Centuries a decline began. The
conflicting doctrines within Tendai philosophy finally produced independent sects.

Shingon Buddhism

Shingon philosophy was founded in the ninth century by Kukai

(774–835 A.D.), known also as Kobo Daishi. The Shingon philosophy of Kukai was a pantheistic mysticism. The universe is considered as the body of the cosmic Buddha Dainichi. The Shingon pantheon included numberless Buddhas, Bodhisattvas, deities, demons, and angels. All phenomena are regarded as activities of Buddha. Shingon Buddhism teaches that wealth, good health, rain, good harvest, and other benefits can be realized through an esoterically adept person.[25]

Kukai borrowed these mystical, cosmological, physical, and psychological speculations from the continent. But Kukai developed his own theory of the ten steps of the spiritual ladder which one must climb to attain enlightenment. They are summarized as follows:

(1) the mind absorbed in thoughts of food and sex, (2) recognition of moral rules and social convention, (3) innocent, childlike belief in a heavenly life, (4) awareness of the reality of existence and the nonentity of self, (5) partial enlightenment through the eradication of self-consciousness, (6) recognition of the oneness of existence and the illusory nature of external existence, (7) enlightenment as to the reality which transcends all relativities, (8) apprehension of the all-embracing "way of reality," (9) recognition of "free movement" in a world of living force, which is neither chaotic mass nor static entity, and (10) true enlightenment through comprehension of the glories of the cosmic mysteries.[26]

Kukai further attempted to unify Buddhism with Shinto. Kukai invented the word "Ryobu Shinto" (Dual Aspect Shinto), which means that Shinto has the dual aspect of Buddhism and Shinto. Shingon Buddhism became popular to the common people through its appeal of esoteric practices such as the incantation of mystic formulae and the promise of worldly profit. Shingon in Japan was similar to Lamaism in Tibet and Mongolia and is the best example of Tantric Buddhism in Japan. Shingon Buddhism influenced the Japanese mentality to appreciate the mystical aspect of spiritual reality.

Amida Buddhism

Among many Buddhist schools, Amida Buddhism or the Pure Land School is one of the most popular schools. In the Twelfth Century Amida Buddhism was wide spread in Japan. According to this Buddhism, one can attain salvation not primarily through one's own effort, but through the grace of and faith in Amida Buddha, who accumulated a vast store of merits in the Pure Land or the Western Heaven, which he can share with the multitudes who pray to him. Although some Buddhists believe that the Amida Buddha was a historical person, it is most likely that he is a mystical figure. It seems that Amida is an abstraction whose principal attribute is infinite mercy.[27]

Honen (1132–1212 A.D.) founded the Jodo (Pure Land) Sect in Japan. During the period of his study on a mountain, he became depressed over the difficulties of attaining enlightenment. Then, he searched for a practical and effective way of universal salvation. He came upon the following passage:

> Whether walking or standing, sitting or lying, only repeat the name of Amida with all your heart. Never cease the practice of it even for a moment. This is the very work which unfailingly issues in salvation for it is accordance with the original vow of that Buddha.[28]

These words were the basis upon which Honen founded the Jodo Sect. Thus, in the Jodo Sect the mere recitation of the name of Amida Buddha is sufficient for salvation, when it is accompanied by faith.

Since the Thirteenth Century, Amida Buddhism has been divided into many sects. It greatly influenced the life and culture of the Japanese people. Amida Buddhism was an "easy way" to salvation, for it did not require long and hard meditation or self-effort, but simple faith in Amida Buddha's grace as sufficient deed for salvation. Thus, it became popular and widespread among the common people. The calling on the name of Buddha *(nembutsu)* is considered sufficient for one's salvation.

Honen's teachings included three basic principles: (1) all may be born into Pure Land Paradise; (2) the incantation of the *nembutsu* requires neither meditation nor intellectual comprehension, but faith only; and (3) that the efficacy of the *nembutsu* is absolute. Honen issued the following statement before his death:

> The method of final salvation that I have taught is neither a sort of meditation such as that practiced by many scholars in China and Japan in the past, nor is it a repetition of the Buddha's name by those who

have studied and understood the deep meaning of it. It is nothing but a mere repetition of the name of the Buddha Amida, without a doubt of his mercy, whereby one may be born into the happiest land of the Buddha.[29]

This statement shows the unique doctrine of Amida Buddhism, that is, salvation by faith alone. It stresses the universality of salvation and the possibility of an easy way to salvation. In the Jodo School, the Amida Buddha is worshipped as the saviour of mankind, and Gautama Buddha is regarded as only a revealer of Amida teachings.

Zen Buddhism

Amida Buddhism was the first major school of Buddhism that developed in Japan in the Twelfth Century. The second major school of Buddhism was Zen Buddhism. Zen Buddhism is perhaps the best known type of Buddhism in the West due to its highly mystical approach to reality. This seems to have an appeal to the modern Western mind, which appears to be tired of its rationalistic approach to life. Zen Buddhism was founded in China in the Sixth Century A.D. by Bodhidharma, an Indian monk. The essence of Zen teaching was included in Gautama Buddha's teachings; but as a definite school it was founded in China. Zen ideas were known in Japan probably during the Nara Period in the Seventh and Eighth Centuries A.D. Zen Buddhism did not flourish in Japan until monk Eisai founded the Rinzai School of Zen in 1191. Shortly afterwards, another monk, Dogen founded the Soto School of Zen. Essentially both schools share similar views. The main difference is that the Soto sect stresses book learning as a supplement to meditation more than the Rinzai sect.[30]

Zen Buddhism stresses silent meditation as the only authentic path and intuitive wisdom which transcends ordinary rationality as the key to enlightenment. It aims at the awakening of the mind or Buddha nature in each person. Faith in a savior and education have no place in Zen. Enlightenment comes only through the immediate and direct intuitive understanding of reality. The following statement depicts the heart of Zen philosophy:

A special transmission outside the Scriptures;
No dependence upon words and letters;

Direct pointing to the soul of man;
Seeing into one's nature and the attainment of Buddhahood.[31]

Zen Buddhism thus emphasizes self-effort for mental discipline more than any other schools. Zen philosophy lays a heavy stresss on the awakening of the Buddha nature in man, which is regarded as a mystical union with reality.

According to D. T. Suzuki, a well-known exponent of Zen in the West, all the philosophy of the East is crystallized in Zen; but this does not mean that Zen is a philosophy in the ordinary sense of the term, for Zen is not a system founded upon logic and analysis. Zen is rather often the antipode of logic, by which Suzuki means the dualistic mode of thinking.[32]

This does not mean that in Zen there is no intellectual element. To achieve some elementary knowledge of the techniques of Zen, one may need some intellectual experience. But Zen Buddhists would insist that one cannot realize the essence of Zen by intellect, reason, or logic. Zen Buddhists would insist that ultimately one must transcend the ordinary framework of rational thinking, if one is to realize the ultimate truth and attain enlightenment.

According to Suzuki, Zen proposes the solution of human problems not by the way of intellectual analysis or book knowledge but by directly appealing to the facts of personal and first hand experiences. Zen explains nothing, but Zen indicates; Zen teaches nothing, but Zen points the way.[33] Hence, there seems to be some anti-intellectual tendency in Zen, at least in the radical claim of Suzuki concerning the essence of Zen.

Zen is also not a religion in the ordinary sense, for Zen has no God to believe in, no rituals to practice, no heaven or paradise to enter. However, Zen does not deny the existence of God. Zen neither denies nor affirms concerning God. Zen seeks to rise above logic and find a higher affirmation where there is no antitheisis.[34] All the pious religious rituals and moral deeds are not essential in Zen. Suzuki asserts, "Zen is the spirit of man."[35] Zen is against all religious conventionalism.

Suzuki claims that Zen is not simply meditation. "Zen purposes to discipline the mind itself, to make it its own master, through an insight into its proper nature."³⁶ Zen does not meditate on such things as the oneness of God or His love. Zen seeks the attainment of freedom of mind. It is against artificial meditation. "Upon what do the fowl of the air meditate? Upon what do the fish in the water meditate? They fly; they swim."³⁷ In like manner, Zen is considered to be an authentic free mode of man's existence.³⁸ Here Zen seems to resemble the Taoist concept of the natural life as the free and authentic life which is in tune and harmony with reality. In this respect Zen might have been influenced by Taoism.

Zen places absolute faith in a man's own inner being. It rejects external authority. It relies entirely upon the authority of man's natural and inner being.³⁹ Zen is a sort of mysticism, which seeks to attain the pure state of union with reality in one's own being.

Zen Buddhism in Japan, however, practices a systematic training of the mind. Zen aims at the realization of its essence in the ordinary daily life of man. Suzuki states that Zen opens a man's eye to the greatest mystery in the daily life, and enables man to embrace the eternity of time and infinity of space. Suzuki claims that these spiritual feats can be achieved "by simply asserting in the most direct way the truth that lies in one's own inner being."⁴⁰

We may question here what is the truth that lies in one's own inner being? How do we know that there is truth within man? How do we know that there is such a thing as eternity of time and infinity of space? Isn't it too subjectivistic to claim that one can attain the authentic existence by simply asserting in the most direct way that truth lies in one's own being? Isn't it too presumptuous and dogmatic to assert that truth lies in man's own inner being? Where is the verifiable evidence to show that man possesses truth in his own being? There seems to be no verifiable and objective answers to these questions, and therefore, it seems that the essence of Zen is subjectivistic. Zen is indeed highly anti-rational and anti-logical.

The techniques of Zen Buddhism may be considered in three key categories: *Zazen, koan,* and *sanzen*. These methods are designed to lead Zen trainees to an enlightenment experience called *satori,* which is the goal in Zen Buddhism.

Zazen literally means "seated meditation." The Zen training usually takes place in a meditation hall. *Zazen* is the basic form of meditation in lotus posture with crossed legs, straight back, and with half open eyes, looking straight ahead. Zen Buddhists sit silently many hours, many days, many years, aiming at the development of their intuitive wisdom.

Koan means problem or riddle on which Zen students meditate. It is a method of testing one's Zen understanding. A *koan* is some statement made by a Zen master, or some answer of his given to a questioner.[41] It is a very important method of Zen training especially in the Rinzai school of Zen, while the Soto school does not practice it.

The following are some example of *koan:*

"We are familar with the sound of two hands clapping. What is the sound of one hand?" (If you protest that one hand can't clap, you go back to the foot of the class. Such a remark simply shows you haven't even begun to get the point.)

"What was the appearance of your face before your ancestors were born?"[42]

"Lo, a cloud of dust is rising from the ocean, and the roaring of the waves is heard over the land."

"Empty-handed I go, and behold the spade is in my hands; I walk on foot, and yet on the back of an ox I am riding; when I pass over the bridge, lo, the water floweth not, but the bridge doth flow."[43]

Admittedly and obviously these statements and questions show that the nature of *koan* is illogical, irrational, and paradoxical. What is the aim of *koan* then? According to Suzuki, the aim of Zen *koan* is that through meditation on *koan* the Zennist may acquire a radically new perspective by which to look into the mysteries of life and the secrets of reality. Zen concludes that the ordinary logical process of reasoning is helpless to give the ultimate answer to our deepest spiritual needs.[44]

The purpose of *koan* is to provoke, excite, baffle, and exhaust the reasoning mind and to destroy the calculating faculty of our being, and to enable man to go beyond the limits of intellectual reasoning. When *koan* exhausts a once rational mind, logic turns into psychology, and reason or intellect surrenders to intuition, according to Zen philosophy.

Sanzen means meditation with consultation. The master gives the Zen disciple a *koan* and the disciple meditates on the *koan* and consults privately with his master usually twice daily. Thus the Zen trainee is not alone, although books and his fellow monks may not help him. The master corrects the inadequate answers, beating down his false conceptions and his prejudices, and also validates the student's correct answer. But Zen insists that when the right answer comes to the student, he usually can recognize it on his own with a sudden force of insight or intuition.[45]

The goal of *zazen, koan* study, and *sanzen* is to lead the student's mind to the awakening stage to acquire intuition, by which the Zennist may realize the nature of the self as reality. This intuitive awakening experience is called *satori*. Though the training may take years, the *satori* experience is a very sudden one like a flash. *Satori* is a sort of preliminary enlightenment. It leads the Zennist to a deeper realization of the self and nature. Zen Buddhists insist that the enlightenment is not an abstract theory, but a concrete reality that must be expressed in the ordinary daily life of the individual in the world.

According to Suzuki, *satori* is "acquiring a new viewpoint."[46] *Satori* is a state or mode of new perspective of the Zennists, in which the habit of logical and rational thinking according to the rules of dualism is destroyed. It is a new viewpoint for looking into the essence of reality. At the *satori* dimension, the Zennist would utter: "All is one, one is none, none is all."[47]

The above statements show that the *satori* experience involves a mystical consciousness of the Zennist. In the *satori* consciousness, the identification of the finite and the infinite takes place, transcending the dualism of the self and other, of good and evil. Nirvana is here in this ordinary world, as the Zennist returns into the world with new perspective. This is an existential dimension of Zen philosophy.

But isn't the identification of the finite and the infinite, of the self and other, and of good and evil, an irrational, absurd, and subjective imagination? The mystical approach to reality in Zen Buddhism has no objective and external basis as a criterion by which we can judge the validity of the Zen thesis. Therefore, how would we know whether the claim of Zen Buddhists concerning the mystical experience of *satori* is right or wrong? How could Zennists verify objectively that the *satori* experience is not a mere subjectivism? Since they discount any value of the ordinary logical reasoning for the Zen experience, and since in fact their aim is to destroy the ordinary way of thinking which involves objective verification with external evidence, it is obvious that the Zennists cannot provide any rational, logical, and objective proof for their claims.

As far as the influence of Zen Buddhism upon the Japanese culture is concerned, there is a wide recognition of its significance.[48] It includes literature (especially short Haiku poems), drama (especially Nō plays), painting (especially brush paintings), Bushido (the Way of the Warrior), archery, Judo, Karate, and the tea ceremony, etc. All these arts and other cultural activities emphasize the concentration of mind toward the identification of mind and object. and the harmony of mind and body.

Nichiren Buddhism

In the Thirteenth Century there was a third major development of Buddhism in Japan, called Nichiren Buddhism. Nichiren (1222–1282) was a dynamic figure and a great reformer.[49] Nichiren viewed sectarian differences of Buddhism as perversions of the original teaching of Buddhism. He regarded the Lotus Sutra as the principal scripture of Buddhism. The Lotus Sutra was written a few centuries after the time of Gautama Buddha. Nichiren desired to return to the religion of Gautama Buddha, but apparently he did not know what pure Buddhism was.

Nichiren attacked all schools of Buddhism, especially Amidaism, because he felt that it should give glory to Gautama Buddha rather than Amida Buddha. Nichiren believed that he was the reincarnation of Bosatsu Jogyo, the disciple of Gautama Buddha. Nichiren had an extreme fanaticism and he regarded himself as the saviour of the nation.

Since the Meiji period in modern Japan, Nichiren made a considerable influence in Japan. He became an object of hero worship. Due to the fanaticism of his followers, Nichiren is an active Buddhist school in Japan, although it is behind Amida, Zen, and Shingon schools in numbers of adherents.

Nichiren doctrines are similar to Tendai doctrines, but the former are narrower and more exclusive than the latter. Nichiren Buddhists worship the eternal Buddha and they believe that when they repeat the sacred formula, "Adoration to the sutra of the lotus of the true law," their souls become identified with the cosmic soul of the eternal Buddha. Thus, the sacred formula is the means of salvation in Nichiren Buddhism. According to Nichiren Buddhism anyone who repeats the sacred formula attains Buddhahood and paradise on earth.[50]

Traditionally religious philosophy dominated the mind and culture of the Japanese people. While the Japanese originally sought the sense of comfort and security on this earth primarily through the Shinto mythology with the blessings and protection of numberless deities, they sought assurance of life-hereafter in many different schools of Buddhism.

The many aspects of Shinto mythology, especially its nationalistic aspect and the idea of the divinity and worship of the emperor, represent the primitive nature of Shinto as an ideology. Many different schools of Buddhism in Japan demonstrate the many contradicting ideas within Buddhist thought, especially between the notion of salvation through grace of and faith in Amida Buddha in the Pure Land School and the notion of enlightenment through meditation and intuition taught in the Zen School.

Since Shinto and Buddhism in Japan do not show any verifiable objective basis for their claim such as historically witnessed revelation, it seems that their ideas are basically human inventions and the products of man's subjectivistic mind. Probably for this reason, many educated Japanese youth are turning away from the mythological Shinto ideas and Buddhist teachings to more rational solutions for their life's quest.

FOOTNOTES

[1]William K. Bunce, *Religions in Japan* (Rutland, Vermont: Charles E. Tuttle Co., 1955), p. 1.

[2]*Ibid.,* pp. 101-102.

[3]Joseph M. Kitagawa, *Religion in Japanese History* (New York: Columbia University Press, 1966), pp. 11-12.

[4]*Ibid.,* p. 12.

[5]*Ibid.*

[6]Bunce, pp. 1-2.

[7]*Ibid.,* p. 2.

[8]Kitagawa, p. 13.

⁹*Ibid.,* pp. 13-14.

¹⁰*Ibid.,* p. 14.

¹¹*Ibid.,* pp. 14-15.

¹²Bunce, p. 108.

¹³Chan, Faruqi, Kitagawa, and Raju, *The Great Asian Religions: An Anthology* (New York: The MacMillan Co., 1969), p. 232.

¹⁴Literally it means "Heavenly Illuminating Great Deity."

¹⁵Bunce, pp. 6-7.

¹⁶*Ibid.,* pp. 108-109.

¹⁷*Ibid.,* pp. 110-111.

¹⁸*Ibid.,* p. 111.

¹⁹This was the period of the Three Kingdoms in Korea: Koguryō, Packche, and Silla.

²⁰Bunce, pp. 45-46.

²¹*Ibid.,* p. 46.

²²Kitagawa, pp. 110ff.

²³Bunce, p. 47.

²⁴*Ibid.,* p. 63.

²⁵*Ibid.,* p. 69.

²⁶*Ibid.,* p. 70.

²⁷Beatrice Suzuki, *Mahayana Buddhism* (New York: Collier Books, 1963), pp. 63ff.

²⁸Bunce, p. 75.

²⁹*Ibid.,* p. 80.

³⁰*Ibid.,* p. 88.

³¹D. T. Suzuki, *Zen Buddhism,* ed. by W. Barrett (Garden City: Doubleday Anchor Books, 1956), p. 9.

³²D. T. Suzuki, *An Introduction to Zen Buddhism* (New York: Grove Press, Inc., 1964), p. 38.

³³*Zen Buddhism,* pp. 7 and 10.

³⁴*An Introduction to Zen Buddhism,* p. 39.

³⁵*Ibid.,* p. 40.

³⁶*Ibid.*

³⁷*Ibid.,* p. 41.

³⁸*Zen Buddhism,* p. 14.

³⁹*Introduction to Zen Buddhism,* p. 44.

⁴⁰*Ibid.,* p. 45.

⁴¹*Zen Buddhism,* p. 134.

⁴²Huston Smith, *The Religions of Man* (New York: Harper and Row, Perennial Library, 1958), p. 146.

⁴³*An Introduction to Zen Buddhism,* pp. 58-59.

⁴⁴*Ibid.,* p. 59.

⁴⁵Smith, p. 148.

⁴⁶*An Introduction to Zen Buddhism,* p. 88ff.

⁴⁷Smith, p. 151.

⁴⁸For more detailed discussion on this topic, see Suzuki, *Zen Buddhism.*

⁴⁹M. Anesaki, *Religious Life of the Japanese People* (Tokyo: The Kokusai Bunka Shinkokai, 1938), p. 54.

⁵⁰Bunce, p. 96.

INDEX